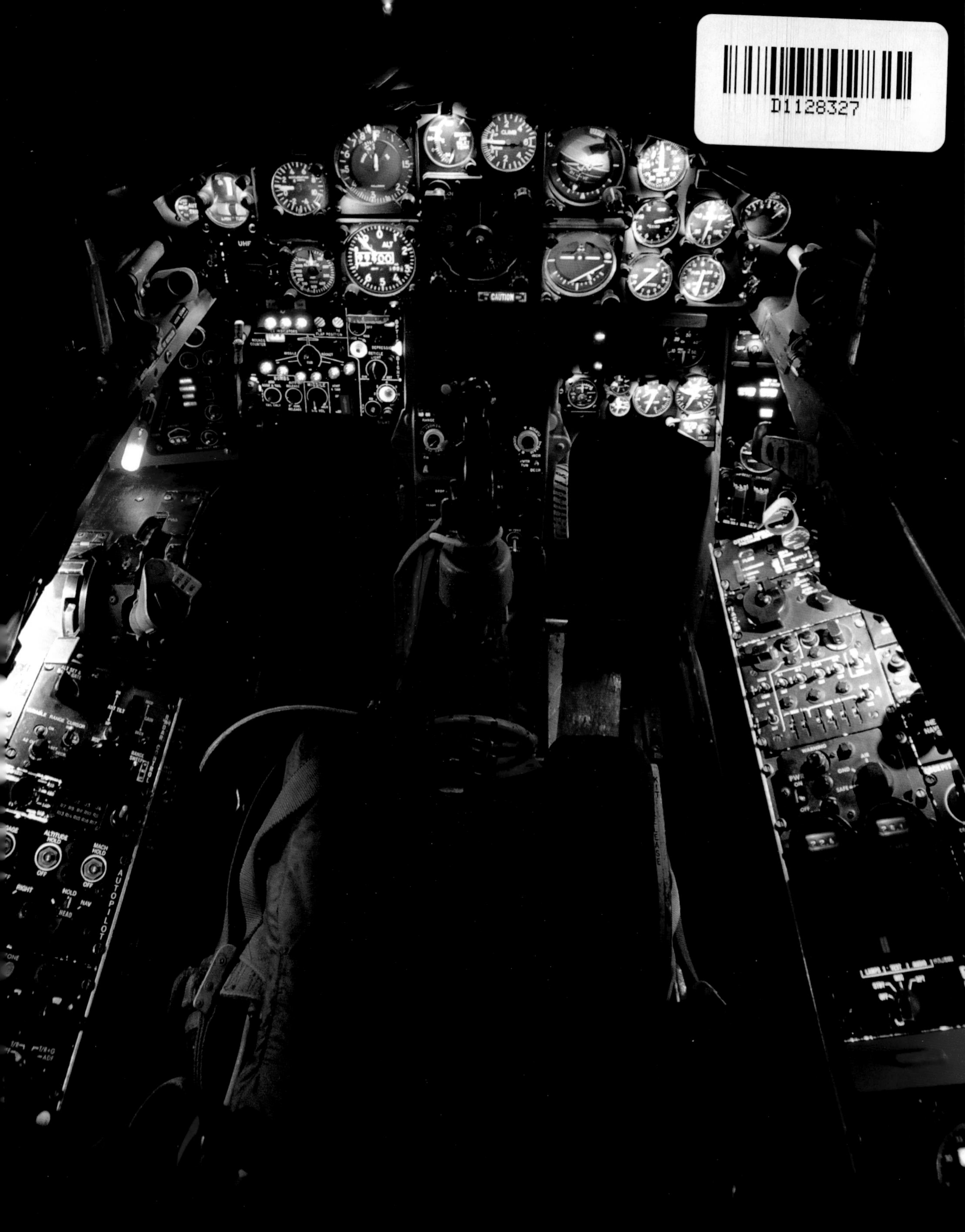
UHF
CAUTION
ALTITUDE HOLD
MACH HOLD
AUTOPILOT
HEATERS

Until the advent of the F-16 Fighting Falcon, the Lockheed F-104G Starfighter international production program was the biggest of its kind. In addition to production lines in the USA, Canada and Japan, at its peak it employed some 60,000 people in factories all over Germany, Belgium, the Netherlands and Italy. Of the 2,575 F-104s built about 2,000 Starfighters would fly above the European continent. The European participants learned a lot from this program, gearing themselves to a type and complexity of production of which they had no previous experience. For the air force pilots the Starfighter surpassed in many respects every other type of aircraft: in speed, ceiling, rate of climb, acceleration and most other aspects of pure performance it had few rivals. And for the aviation enthusiasts no other military aeroplane could touch its sheer glamour. In Europe the Lockheed F-104 Starfighter still enjoys the same cult status as the Grumman F-14 Tomcat does in the United States.

Yet the Starfighter, while clever and advanced, was also a remarkably solid and simple aircraft, as the two authors of this book found time and again during their research through the whole set of maintenance manuals. The task of finding the most interesting information was a time consuming — but very interesting — job as was going through several thousand digital pictures to find the best images for this book. 'Uncovering the Lockheed (T)F-104G Starfighter' is indeed the result of a lifelong passion of both authors for this wonderful aircraft. Three years have been spent in photographing over forty F-104s all over Europe, some perfectly preserved, some patiently being restored, others ready to be scrapped tracking all the subtle differences between the various types. It is intended as a proud successor to the original F-104G bible, the Verlinden Publications Lock On No.1, researched and written by Willy Peeters and published thirty years ago.

This book would not have been realised without the help of many people, and our thanks also go to the people behind the Technical schools of Lechfeld, Büchel, Erding & Saffraanberg, the restoration groups of Volkel & Memmingen, the aviation museums of Brussels, Beauvechain, Soesterberg, Aviodrome, Berlin, München, Wernigerode, Niederalteich, Speyer, Altenburg-Nobitz, Koblenz & Oslo and the various photographers who made their slide collections available. Big thanks to Jim Rotramel for verifying all captions, Piet Snijders for his F-104G scale drawings and Willy Peeters for the cockpit diagrams. Our special thanks go to Lex van Beek, curator of the aircraft in depot of the Soesterberg museum, Theo Stoelinga for additional caption information and Johan Bringmans for his insight in the Starfighter, his help with the captions, his maintenance manuals, his picture collection.   To all of you: *THANKS GUYS!*
Danny Coremans & Peter Gordts

All pictures by Danny Coremans, unless otherwise specified
Captions by Peter Gordts and Danny Coremans
Text corrections by Jim Rotramel
Layout by Danny Coremans and Peter Gordts
Photo preparation and pre-press by Danny Coremans

© 2012 by DACO Publication
Antwerpen, Belgium
Printed in Belgium
ISBN: 9789080674707
Suggested Retail Price: 34,75 Eu

The pitot tube of the F-104 consists of a hollow mast attached to the radome and the heated anti-ice coil pitot head. The radome is manufactured by weaving fiberglass strands, pulled through a resin bath, under regulated tension around a cone-like steel tool. After curing, the cone is milled precisely on the inside and outside to exact dimensions. The Tech Manual stipulates FS16473 as colour for the radome, and FS34079 for the antiglare area, but it's wise to use a lighter version on a scale model.

Once unlocked the radome slides forward on a rail system. Once against the forward stop, technicians can access the main section of the radar without having to remove the radome. Upon release of the forward stop lock, the radome can be completely removed from the nose section.

The NASARR all weather radar features a moving disc able to look up, down and either side of the aircraft to a certain angle. The radar weighs in quite heavy and helps counterbalance the whole aircraft which otherwise would be tailheavy. The sand-coloured foam around the protruding feedhorn forward of the dish helps to separate the outgoing and incoming radar signals.

All (T)F-104Gs are fitted with a small window at the base of the windscreen. The Shooting Range computer searches and tracks the radiant heat of targets through this glass window by means of infrared and supplies data to the AIM-9 Sidewinders. Starfighters operating primarily for ground attack often have this window blanked off with a metal plate to eliminate chipping and other FOD damage.

Note the Rain Removal nozzle cover in closed position, located in front of the left plexiglass. The Rain Removal System is designed to clear the left windshield panel of rain by directing a blast of hot engine bleed air from a series of small holes in the aft face of the nozzle. The nozzle is spring-loaded to the closed position and is raised by bleed air pressure.

A canopy jettison handle is provided on the left side of the cockpit to free the pilot when faced with a ground emergency. A single press of the release button opens a spring-loaded hatch revealing a simple T-handle. The handle connects to a 1,8 meter (6 feet) long cable that keeps the rescuer at a safe distance from the canopy jettison pyrotechnics.

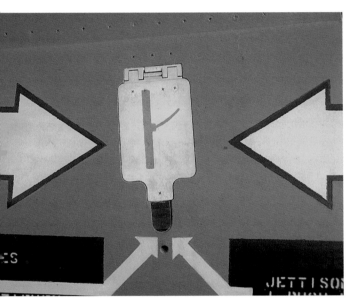

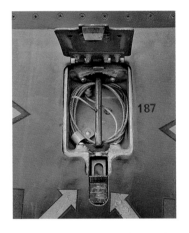

Below: the Angle of Attack transducer on the left side of the fuselage is connected to the AoA indicator in the cockpit and also commands the stick shaker system. A similar AoA transducer on the right side commands the stick kicker.

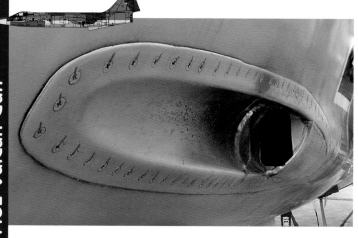

On the left side of the single-seater is the blast tube for the internal M61 Vulcan cannon.

The rectangular shaped aperture in the muzzle cover is big enough to allow the very fast rotating barrels to pass up to one hundred 20 mm electrically primed rounds per second. Once in a while it goes wrong and a ricochet - a rebouncing bullet - damages the fuselage, or in worst case: enters the air intake and shatters the engine blades

Access to the gun compartment is provided by a big panel and a door. The panel, covering the forward part of the compartment (picture below left shows its internal side), is only detached for boresighting or removing the gun. The door covers the aft part of the compartment and hinges down for gun servicing, such as bolt removal and ammunition loading. Note the boresight chart on the inside of the door with all info necessary to align the gun barrels and the gunsight in the cockpit.

On RF-104Gs the gunnery equipment is removed and in its place extended-range fuel tanks are installed as well as provisions for the internal camera systems. In that case the shroud for the blast tube is sealed by a bolt-on cover plate, part of a from-gun-to-fuel tanks conversion kit.

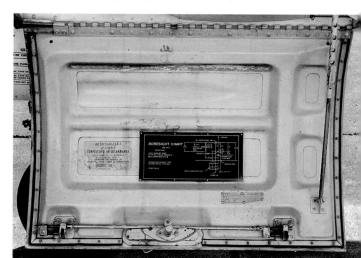

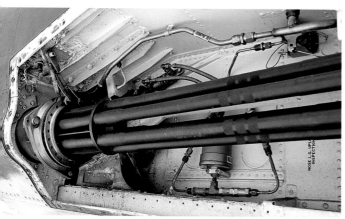

© Pierre Schaffrath

The M61 Vulcan is an electric operated six-barreled rotary-fire cannon. The gun's rate of fire, selectable between 65 or 100 rounds per second, gives the pilot a shot density that will enable a 'kill' even when fired in less-than-one-second bursts.

© Pierre Schaffrath

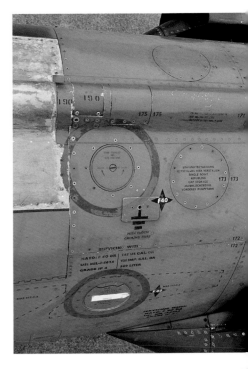

All F-104Gs incorporate a single point high-pressure refueling system that refuels all tanks. Alternatively the Starfighter can also be refueled by gravity at two places, the first being identified by the second red circle close to the spine. The dotted lines in this area denote the location of the bolt-on air-refueling probe, which in the case of the F-104G has never been fitted. Transfers to a particular fuel tank is selected through the Master Precheck & Refueling Switch Panel, located under door 179 which is opened on r/h photo. Left picture shows part of the additional fuel tank that Recce RF-104Gs have installed in the gun compartment.

FX52

The right hand sided AoA transducer for the stick's kicker system is mounted more forward towards the nose cone than the stick's shaker transducer on the left hand fuselage side.

Pushing this external detent allows the External Canopy Release Handle to spring out of its slot and into operating position. Turning the handle clockwise unlatches and raises the canopy slightly off the right hand sill and from this point it can be opened manually.

To close, the canopy is lowered manually to the top of the lift cams. The External Canopy Release Handle is then rotated counterclockwise over the black painted line, which in turn will fully lower and latch the canopy. The handle is then rotated halfway back to the slot and secured under the detent.

11

The temperature probe is located just in front of the Electrical Load Center Bay.

The air scoop integrated in the Electrical Load Center Bay access door supplies cooling air for the radar and the computers of the aft electronic compartment, which is located above the circuit breaker bay. The internal shape of its channel can be seen on next page's bottom picture.

In case of hydraulic or electrical failure the pilot can manually open the spring-loaded Ram Air Turbine into the airstream, driving an emergency generator and hydraulic pump. Once extended, it cannot be retracted in flight.

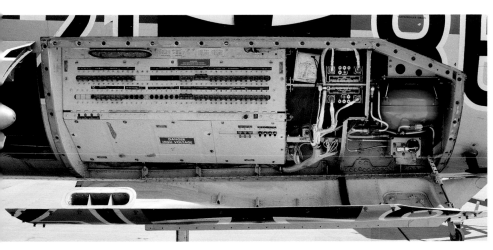

The Electrical Load Center Bay with the main circuit breakers' box. Two emergency batteries and a set of voltage regulators are placed to the left of the LOX bottle. This converter bottle contains five liters of Liquid Oxygen, sufficient for approximately four hours. The large door swings open to allow access for maintenance and/or to supply external cooling air directly to the aft electronics compartment.

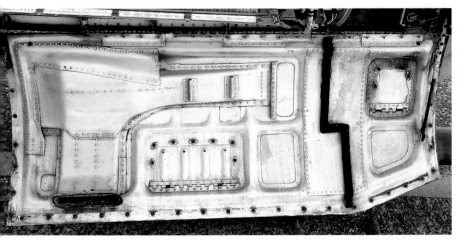

© Hubert Van Acker

13

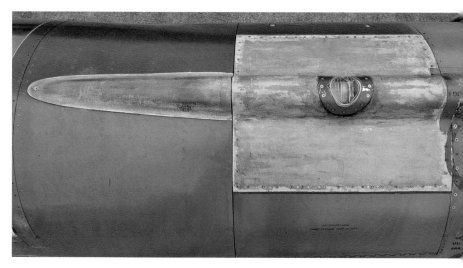

© Johan Bringmans

The fibre-coloured panels on the spine, situated just behind the cockpit, are the flush-fitting top antennas for the IFF (wig shaped) and the UHF radio (square). A white anti-collision light is integrated in the UHF antenna.

The air conditioning unit incorporates a water boiler which is serviced with distilled water through an open vent located on the right side just below the computer hatch.

Note below the small NACA scoop, an item peculiar to Dutch Volkel-based F-104G on the left hand side just below this antenna panel. It directs cooling air to the ECM equipment, which is installed in a converted Ammunition Container.

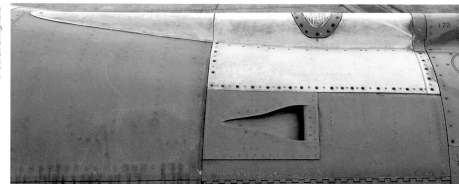

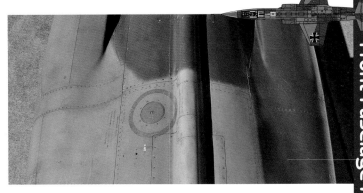

The red circle on the foreground of the left picture denotes the forward filler point for the gravity refueling of the internal fuel tanks. A similar (occasionally red painted) filler cap for the aft filler point is situated further down the spine. Upper views of typical F-104 intakes show the spacing between them and the fuselage to separate turbulent boundary layer air from the engine intakes.

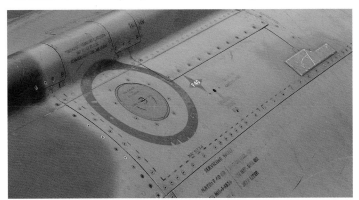

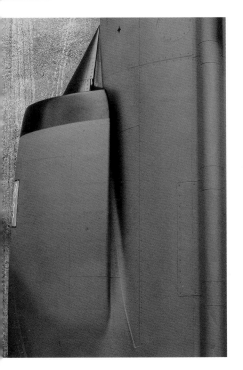

15

The typical air intake with the non-moving supersonic shock wave suppression cones. Initially the Starfighters intake lips and intake cones were covered in black Spraymate electro-thermal paint to prevent icing. These parts soon proved not to be affected by ice and the anti-icing paint was deleted.

Note the bleed slot just aft of the cone, which enables shockwave dissipation and channels cooling air around the engine inside the fuselage.

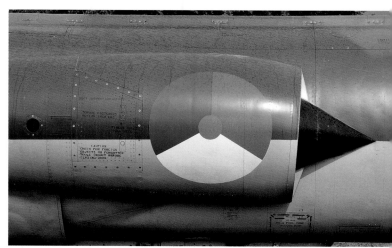

The inlet duct access doors, below right in open position, allow easy inspection of the engine's compressor first stage. On bare-metal schemes this access door has its edges painted with grey anti-corrosion paint.

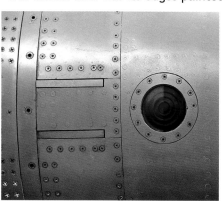

The little red vane sticking out of the spine is part of the engine oil level dipstick, indicating in a glimpse that the dipstick is not secured properly.

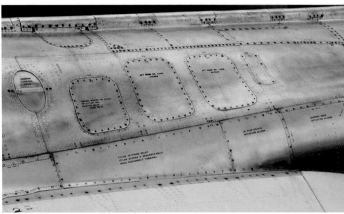

The wing-to-fuselage panels cover the electrical Leading Edge Flap Actuator, the five wing spars and the Trailing Edge Flap Actuator. The cutaway picture shows the location of the aft main saddle fuel bladder cells, accessible through two access panels on either side of the fuselage. The slightly smaller panel covers the control rigging pin and auto pilot actuator-aileron. For all ground running and take-off conditions, the supply of additional cooling airflow is provided by eight sets of inward opening doors, two of these are the oval shaped springloaded flaps located aside the access panels.

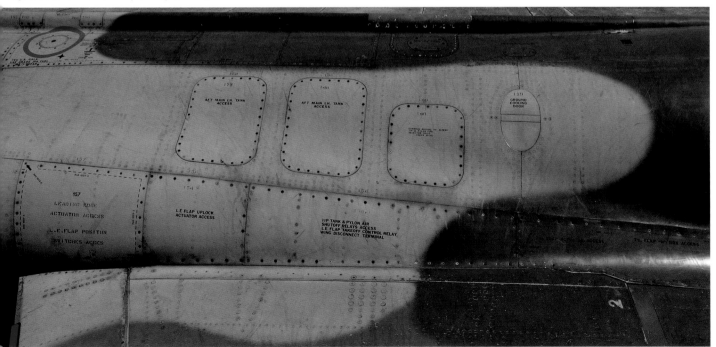

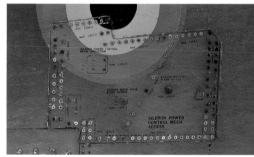

The design of the F-104's wings caused quite a stir in its day, with its narrow span, thin chord and extremely sharp leading edge. The flaps and slats are electrically operated whilst the ailerons are operated using the aircrafts 3000 PSI hydraulic system. The only access panel on the top of the wing allows inspection of these aileron hydraulic power controls.

Note the lack of rivet dents on the wing surface. All rivets are carefully puttied over in the factory to assure a smooth airflow.

The sharp wing edges are protected by U-shaped covers to prevent personnel injuries.

On the right hand photo you see the Boundary Layer Control (BLC) duct in detail, normally covered by the trailing edge flap. Flap selection for landing automatically directs engine air from the 17th compressor stage to the BLC valves just in front of and on top of the trailing edge flaps.
This `blown flaps` system generates extra lift, permitting lower landing speeds.

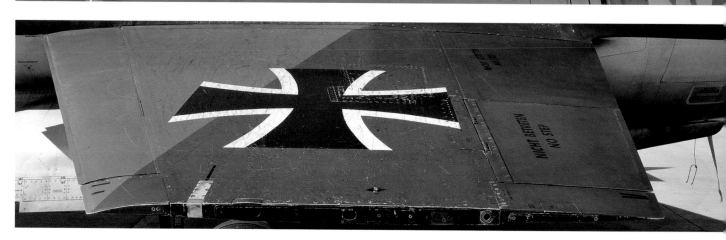

The F-104's famous wing is less than 5 cm / 2" thick at its tips. Wingtip external stores for the F-104 are either fuel tanks or missile rails. These slide over the wingtip and are aligned using the different black stripe markings. The holes are provisions to attach these stores to the wings. Although seldom seen as such, the Starfighter can fly clean without wingtip-mounted stores. For this configuration small wingtip lights are provided, red on the left wing and a greenish-blue on the right wing.

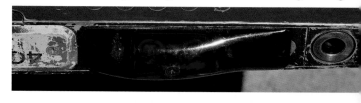

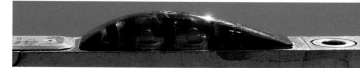

The Red Dog wingtip missile launcher overlaps the wingtips through a wing-shaped well inside the launcher. The one-piece launcher rail is made from high strength aluminium alloy and its flanges are slotted at three places so that the missile's lugs can be inserted. The complete trailing edge section consists of a transparent coloured plastic navigation light.

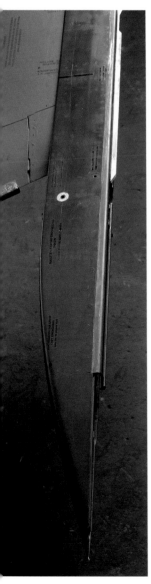

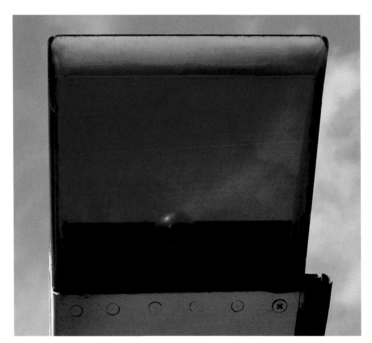

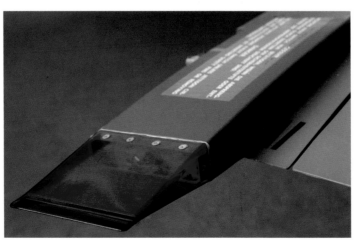

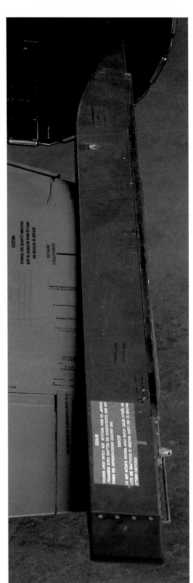

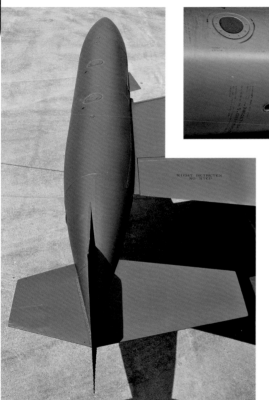

Each wing tip can carry an external tank containing 1287 liters or 170 gal of fuel. It is serviced from the single-point pressure filler system at the fuselage or individually by gravity through the two filler units on the top of each tank and can be jettisoned in case of emergency.
Note the asymmetrical shaped inboard fin of the tip tank versus the other fins and the integrated navigation light glass on the outboard side. Note also the downward angle of the underwing pylon tank on the top picture.

A small 'eyebrow' streak located just above the leading edge flap eliminates potential tank flutter and aids a clean wing-tank separation in case of jettisoning.

The tiptank has a 16,5 cm - 6 $1/2$ inch deep recessed well, clearly visible on the photo below, in which the wing tip is encased.

Internal pumps, piping and sectional walls become visible on this cut-out fuel tank.

23

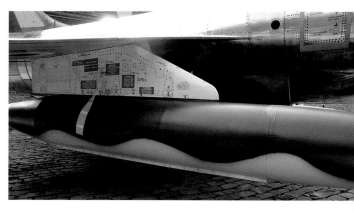

© Luc Van den Ende

The F-104 standard pylon tank can carry 740 liters / 195 gallons of fuel, and the so-called 'combat' pylon tank 870 l / 230 gal. Just as the tip tank, the pylon tank is fitted with the necessary plumbing for transferring fuel to the fuselage aft centre tank. The plumbing in the 'combat' tank is simplified and the internal strengthening is replaced by an external lateral stiffening bar on the lower-right hand side only, as can be seen on the upper right picture. No fuel quantity indicating system or low level float switch is provided in these tanks, resulting in space for these extra liters of fuel. The circular access panels are omitted as well.

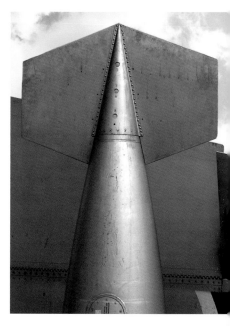

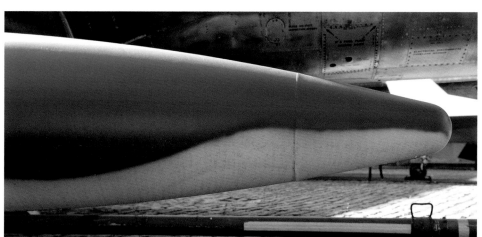

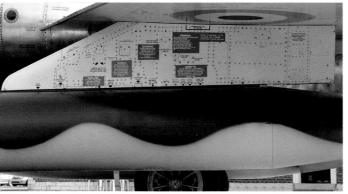

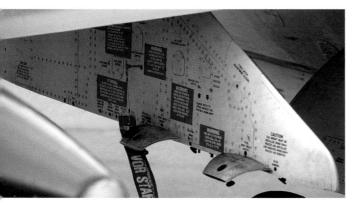

The wing pylon is designed to carry fuel tanks as well as ordnance. Two sway braces provide stability when rocket pods or bombs are attached. Note that the F-104G pylon is vertical towards the horizon.

The F-104`s external fuel tanks can be jettisoned if required, with pyrotechnic charges pushing the tiptanks sideways and the underwing tank / pylon assembly pushed downwards to clear the aircraft.

Below: the pylon attachment explosive bolt assembly sticking through the wing's upper surface is normally covered.

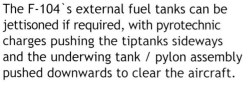

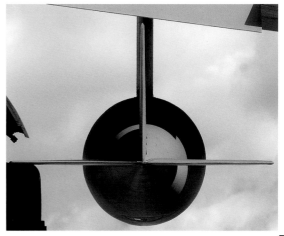

25

The J79 engine's front casing is cast magnesium-thorium and thus emits alpha radiation, which is a serious medical hazard if one is repeatedly exposed to its dust or fumes. For that reason, some F-104s briefly wore telltale yellow-red radiation warning signs on the right hand side in the area between the rectangular ground cooling door and the oval ground cooling/fire access door.

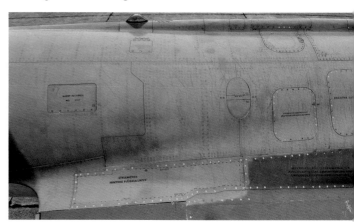

All around the F-104's fuselage, in the region of the engine's first compressor stage, eight 'suck-in' oval and rectangular shaped inlet doors supply secondary air for cooling as well as to ventilate the engine bay. These are also used for fire access directly into this area.

Starfighters in German service have a red teardrop shaped anti-collision beacon mounted on the spine.

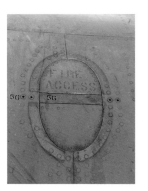

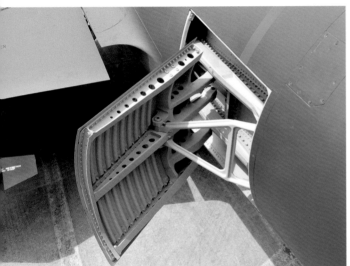

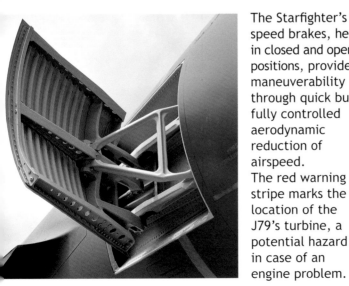

The Starfighter's speed brakes, here in closed and open positions, provide maneuverability through quick but fully controlled aerodynamic reduction of airspeed.
The red warning stripe marks the location of the J79's turbine, a potential hazard in case of an engine problem.

The removable aft fuselage part fits around the J79's afterburner section. Natural metal examples show the various metal hues as well as the effect of the spot welding. The dull grey skin parts are made of pure titanium, the shiny of stainless steel. The cone part above the exhaust is made of highly ductile titanium. Like on the wings surface, no deep rivet dents are found here.

Note the upper and lower navigation lights, orange on top, white on the undersides.

Right of the Decimomannu zap is the thin aluminium foil cover for the ejectable LEADS 200 Flight Data Recorder, which about 50 Luftwaffe F-104s are retrofitted with by the end of the seventies.
The recorder, located behind the MB ejection seat, uses a C120 BASF Chrome Dioxide CrO_2 cassette, similar to those for home music recording.

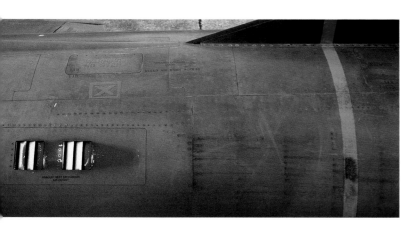

The six louvers on the left hand side of the fuselage are exhaust for the engine bleed air. Below: the navigation lights flashed off and on. Note the blackouts — in the shape of a slice of cake in the orange light and a crescent in the white – directed toward the cockpit to prevent blinding of the pilot when 'checking six' in his mirrors.

© Luc Van den Ende

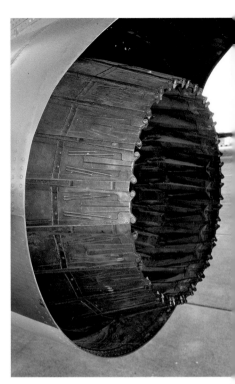

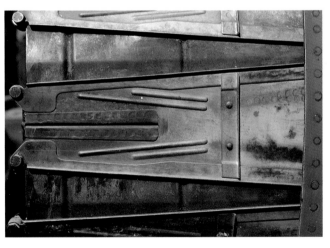

The original J79-GE-11A exhaust nozzle in the open (left) and closed (right) positions.

The closed position provides the most performance without using the afterburner. The nozzle fully opens during afterburner use.

An emergency handle in the cockpit allows the pilot to close the nozzle in case of closure failure.

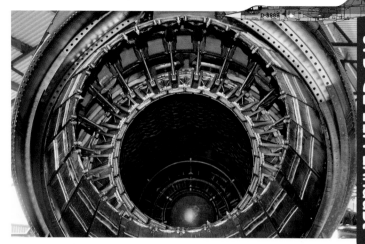

The inside of the exhaust nozzle petals as well as a look into the afterburner section, showing the rear cone and the flame holder mounted around it. By-pass air around the engine, entering the afterburner pipe through hundreds of louvers, keeps the temperature under control and protects the fuselage structure against the heat of the AB. The picture below right shows the torch igniter through which an intense flame fires up the afterburner.

During the early '70s the Germans retrofitted their F104's with upgraded engines, developed by the Motor und Turbinen-Union and designated J79-MTU-J1K. These can be recognized from their less complicated afterburner variable exhaust nozzles. This particular version produces more thrust than the original J79-GE-11A, burns its fuel more economically and emits much less tell tale smoke. As with the original GE-11A exhaust, the MTU-J1K has a variable nozzle system as shown above (open) and below (closed). A malfunction in this system would cause the nozzle to move to its full open position, resulting in a severe loss of thrust. Therefore an emergency nozzle closure system is provided so that the nozzle can be closed and thrust regained by pulling a T-handle in the cockpit, connected to the nozzle by flexible cable.

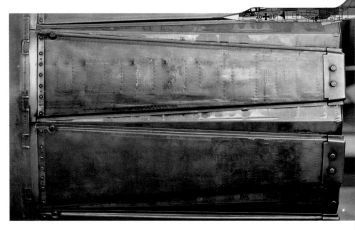

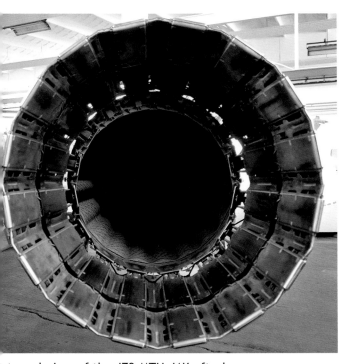

Internal view of the J79-MTU-J1K afterburner. The inner rear cone sports a ceramic coating to protect it against extreme temperatures. Note that the position of the torch igniter has been moved from the bottom to the top of the flame holder, compared to the J79-GE-11A.

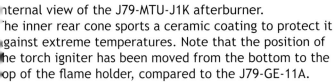

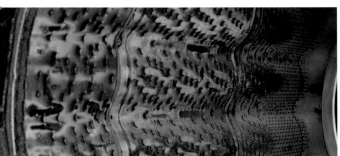

STABILATOR-HORN

STAB.
NEUTRALPOSITION

NAS 1203-3

NAS 1203-1
NAS 1203-8
NAS 1203-6

BEI STARTSTELLUNG MUSS
DIE VORDERKANTE INNERHALB
DER MARKIERUNG STEHEN!

FOR TAKE OFF TRIM LEADING
EDGE MUST LIE WITHIN MARKER

NAS 1203-4

82
82

2

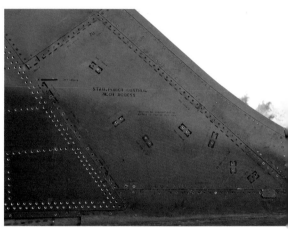

STAB. POWER CONTROL
PITCH ACCESS

FX 21

FX 15

Characteristic for the F-104 is the rhombic one-part-all-moving horizontal stabilizer mounted on top of the vertical tail. It's also its Achilles heel, while flying with a high angle of attack there's a risk of the main wings blanking off the air flow over the stabilizer, resulting in loss of lift over its surface and followed by sudden airplane pitch-up and loss of control. To prevent angle-of-attack induced loss of control, the Automatic Pitch Control (APC) system activates a critical AoA (as sensed by the left AoA transducer) to set off the stick shaker, a very noticeable fore and aft movement of the control stick in the cockpit. If the pilot ignores this warning and AoA continues to increase until the kicker cuts in (activated by the right AoA transducer), automatically forcing the control stick violently forward to lower the nose to an acceptable AoA.

The stabilizer movement is restricted to 5° up and 17° down (thick white line), while the take off position at 5° down is being marked by the T-mark (sometimes extended by a thin white line as seen on the top picture).

Bare metal F-104s are usually not as shiny as the example above, nor is the rudder as wrinkled. Two large magnesium panels, covering the stabilizer actuators & servo assembly from both sides of the fin, are painted light grey on bare metal Zippers to prevent corrosion. Note the subtle differences between the left side access panel (only) on Fokker (top inset) and Lockheed (above) / Sabca (below) built Starfighters, with the Fokker lacking the four circular panels giving direct access to the hydraulic actuators and their filters. The tail beam is made out of forged metal and normally also painted light grey. On 63-13243 this beam and rudder panels are painted in German colours. The small inset picture below shows the hydraulic fitting connections for the actuators of the rudder and stabilizer, which need to be disconnected before the tail section is removed from the fuselage. To avoid jamming of the rudder caused by expansion of the heat resistant stainless steel plating of the tail cone assembly due to engine heat, a rather big wedge is left between the fairing and the rudder.

35

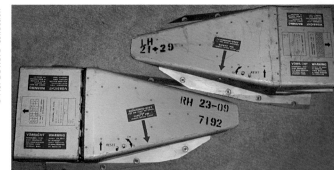

© Flor De Neve collection

Between 1982 and '84, almost at the final years of their carreer, all German Marine F-104Gs were equipped with the Tracor built AN/ALE-40(N) Counter Measure Dispenser System (CMDS) in the 4 and 8 o'clock positions. This gives the Naval Zipper driver a means to defeat infrared seeking anti-aircraft missiles and radar by ejecting magnesium flares and/or thousands of tiny strands of aluminum foil cut to different lengths to match the various wavelengths of the enemy's commonly used radars. The right side dispenser accommodates fifteen 25 x 52 x 205 mm, 370 gr MJU-7A/B infrared decoy flares while the left side dispenser holds thirty 25 x 25 x 207 mm 180 gram RR-170A/AL chaff cartridges.

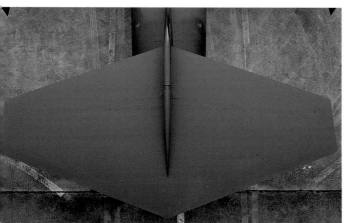

The horizontal stabilizer is a full cantilever semi-monocoque structure consisting of a forged full aluminum alloy span main spar beam and conventional sheet metal skin supported by stamped metal ribs.
Note the uncovered stabilizer actuator beam and its two pushrods on the top picture.

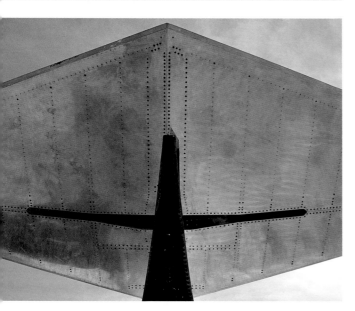

"DPM Library"

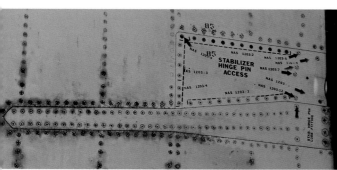

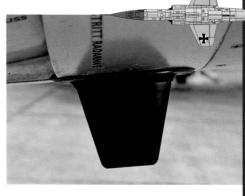

Views of the twin radar compartment cooling exhausts on the F-104's belly, just behind the radome. The small black antenna is part of the TACAN (TACtical Air Navigation) system.

Note the jacking, hoist and mooring markings — all three just below the bushing which is used for the adapter as shown on the bottom left two pictures.

The brown square on the cockpit access hatch is an UHF radio antenna.

Below right are the two front ECM fairings installed on RNAF Volkel based F-104s near the end of their service years. It's an ECM system based on the AN/ALQ-126A, used to counter surface threats such as semi-active radar guided SAMs.

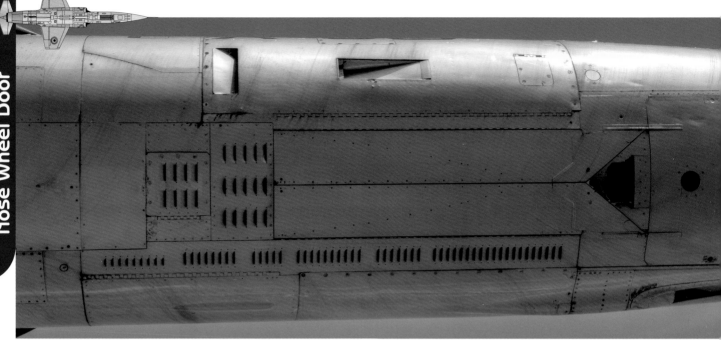

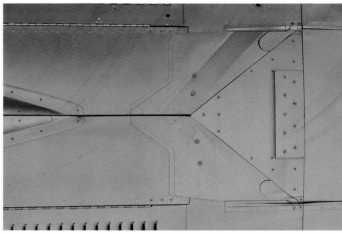

Just in front of the nose wheel bay is the Vulcan's muzzle gas exhaust duct that allows hot gasses to escape.
Exhausted soot creates the typical dirt streaks seen on the nose gear doors after firing the cannon.
The picture above is of a RF-104G, and as the recce bird is not fitted with a cannon, there's no muzzle duct either.

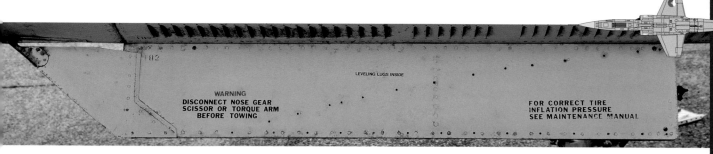

The original straight-edged nose gear doors of the early F-104 models have been extended with a triangular arrestor cable or barrier net deflector on the F-104G. It's hinged at the front tip edge. Note the series of pre-drilled holes, found on all single seater F-104G nose wheel doors, to which the bulged fairings over the internal cameras on the RF-104G are attached (see page 46-47).

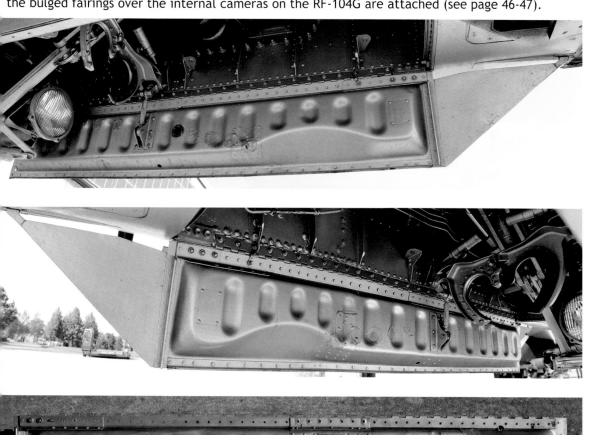

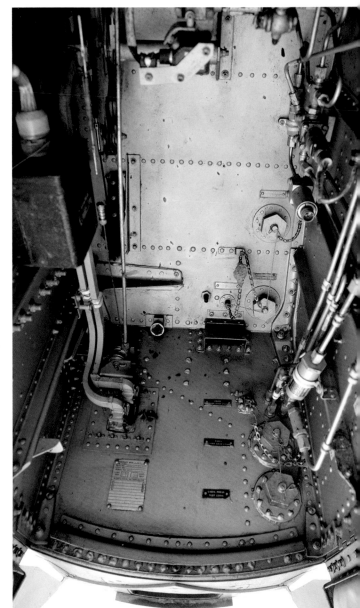

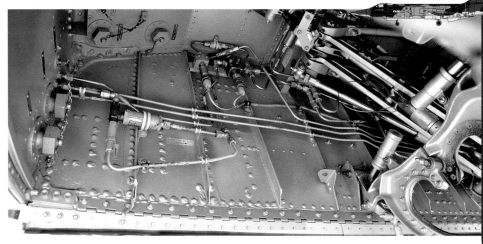

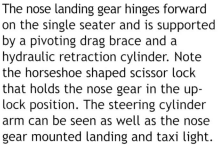

The nose landing gear hinges forward on the single seater and is supported by a pivoting drag brace and a hydraulic retraction cylinder. Note the horseshoe shaped scissor lock that holds the nose gear in the up-lock position. The steering cylinder arm can be seen as well as the nose gear mounted landing and taxi light.

The F-104 nose wheel comes with spooked or flat hubs, regardless of tire size. The scissor link connects the steering collar on the upper section of the gear to the moveable lower section, allowing for steering. The scissor link can be disconnected on top to allow towing. The tow bar pins fit into the axle centre holes.

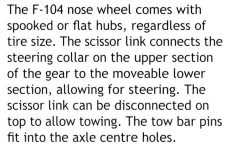

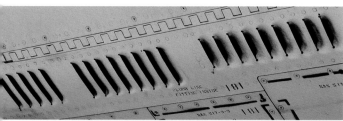

The longitudinal louvers along the well vents the cooling, purge and bleed air coming from the cannon bay.

When the trigger is pressed, engine bleed air streams into the gun compartment purge ducts. It's directed aft into the gun housing and spent cartridge stowage compartment to expel explosive gases. This action continues 12.5 seconds after the trigger has been released.

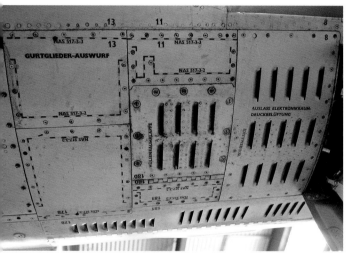

These gasses from the cartridge stowage compartment are dispelled through the two sets of louvers just aft of the nose wheel well.

The pictures left and right show the ammunition link ejector guide. The belted ammunition is routed from the ammunition box into the Vulcan gun feeder where the iron links are stripped from the rounds. On certain Starfighters (e.g. Belgian, and German till 1967) these links are ejected overboard. The external guide prevents ingestion of these links in the engine intake. On all other F-104Gs the gun feeder ejects the stripped links into the cartridge bay where they are stowed together with the empty cartridge shells. In this case there's no link ejector guide installed (see photo above left).

© Luc Van den Ende

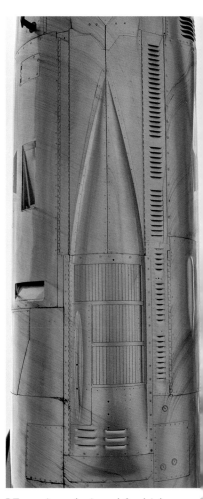

© Joop Dionet

A bulged cover under the F-104's belly behind the front landing gear bay is typical for the RF version, designed for high speed low-level photo-recon missions. To open the camera cover, the scissor link on the nose landing gear has to be disconnected and the nose wheel turned 90°. The RF-104G's three identical TA-7M cameras, made by De Oude Delft in Holland, are mounted in tandem in a right oblique (70 mm lens), vertical (52 mm) and left oblique (70 mm) configuration on a common rack in the original shell case stowage compartment. Thirty meters of film are good for a grand total of 450 57 x 57 mm negatives.

In the late 1970s the German Navy installed a modernized reconnaissance system in their RF-104Gs. A more bulbous looking cover is the clue to differentiate the new low-altitude KRb 6/24 camera/infrared camera RS-710 sensor installation in the lower camera bay from the early '70s triple photo camera configuration as shown on the previous page. The infrared sensor takes pictures at night and in poor visibility and gives the RF-104G a limited all-weather capability.

Another clue to modified Marine RF-104G is the small window in the left fuselage side. It covers a longer focal length KS-87B oblique camera mounted in the upper camera bay, which was created by removing again the ammunition bay fuel tank installed in the early RF-104Gs.

Five panels on the belly give access to the fuel pumps located at the bottom of the internal fuel tanks. Excess bleed air coming from the slot inside the air intakes is dumped through two vents.

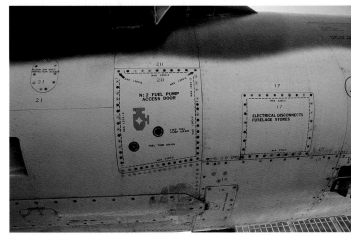

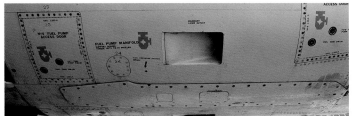

The centerline pylon, used for carrying bombs, bomb dispensers, reconnaissance & travel pods or a nuclear weapon, fits into a large bay and only the lower part remains visible. This bay concept allows space for the release components whilst creating enough ground clearance for the stores. The large bay is covered when the pylon is not installed (see previous page above right).

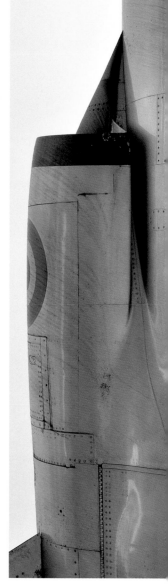

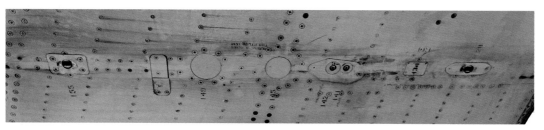

The typical F-104 wing design shown to good effect. The wings underside shows in the center the location of the underwing pylon attachment bolts and its fuel and electrical connection points.

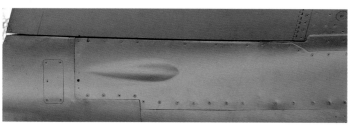

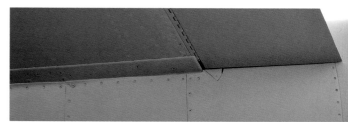

The tip of the air intake cone touches the fuselage and tapers further aft. This is to reduce the disturbing influence of fuselage boundary air to the engine intake.

The leading edge and trailing edge flaps are piano hinged.

A small bulge on the aft area of the wing root panels covers the trailing edge flap actuator. These bulges are a necessity due to the lack of space inside the wing root.

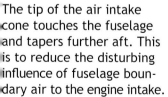

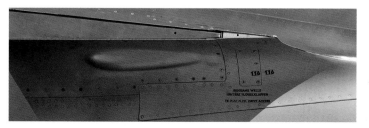

The main gear leg on the (T)F-104G is sturdier than the preceding Starfighter models to accommodate heavier loadings in the fighter-bomber role when compared to its original interceptor mission. The change is subtle and only visible from the underside. The ring on the landing leg is used as mooring point to anchor the aircraft or for towing by cable.

The main gear leg is hinged at the centerline keelbeam and supported by a high-pressure nitrogen-oil shock absorber. A mechanical link with the leg holds the aft gear door open. A cleverly engineered articulating set of rods and levers mounted on the front end of the main gear leg folds the wheel 90° inwards, allowing the assembly to fit in the shallow wheel bays.

The main wheel incorporates a multi-disk brake unit. The tire and rim of the European fighter-bomber / interceptor G-models is noticeably wider than on all other models, like the A/C, B/D/F, CF & J. The reinforced spiked rim allows the heavier weight of the (T)F-104G.
Also note the vertical hinge connecting the wheel to the landing gear leg and the linkage to turn the wheel 90° so it can stored into the wheelbay.

© Luc Janssen

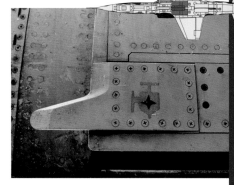

The forward main landing gear doors are fitted with a corner hook to catch emergency barrier nets on runways to avoid damage to the landing gear.

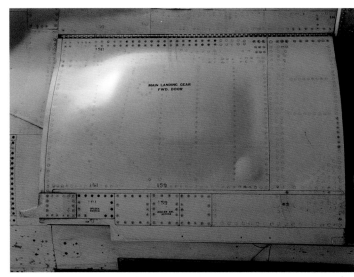

The front doors remain partially open when the landing gear is extended due to interference with the drag strut cylinders.

Another feature on the (T)F-104G in comparison to earlier models is the semi-rounded (and notoriously difficult to capture on photographs) external bulge to accommodate its wider wheels.

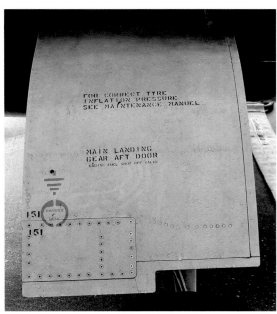

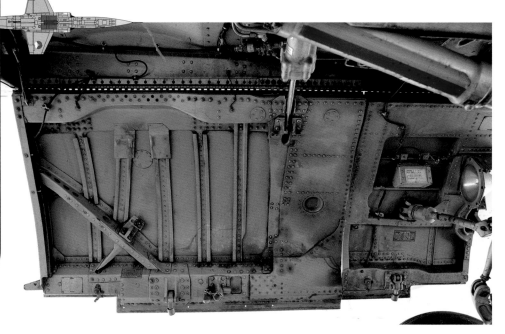

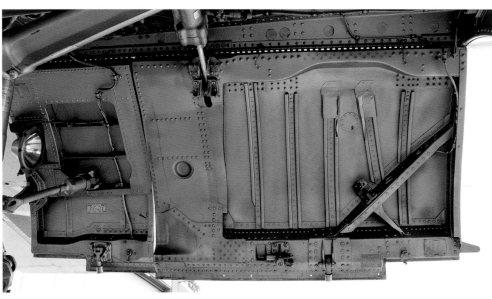

In flight the main gear doors are hydraulically operated. On the ground they can be pulled open by hand for access to and inspection of the gear wells. The aft landing gear doors each hold a landing light. The red marked flat spike on the trailing edge aids to a jamming-free closure of this door.

Unobstructed view of the front part of the large landing gear bay, an unusual situation as the main doors hide this area most of the time. The red stripes on the drag strut retraction cylinder and the black stripes are alignment reference lines when adjusting the landing gear links.

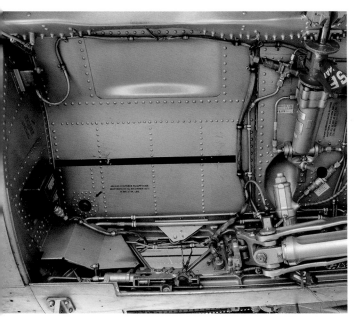

With the main doors still fully opened, the large drag strut retraction cylinders of the main landing gear, the drag brace and over-centre link, all the hydraulic tubes and the occasional electrical wiring are clearly visible. Hydraulic tubes are easily identifiable by standard NATO coded blue/yellow stickers wrapped around them.

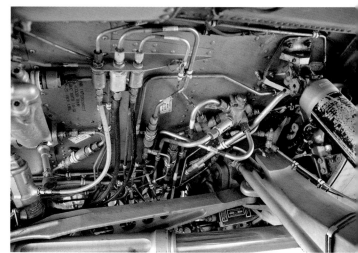

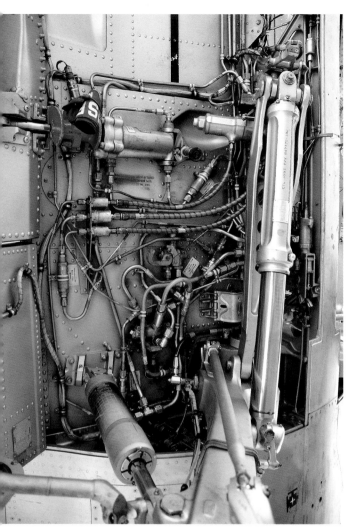

The myriad of hydraulic tubes running along the wheel well upper walls are for the gear extension and retraction cycle components as well as for the brakes. The red clamps on the door actuators prevent closure of the heavy doors by gravity while maintenance is performed or while the Crew-Chief checks this area for hydraulic leaks.

Picture below right shows the reason why the main doors remains slightly open when the MLG is extended: despite the already integrated cut-outs the door's aft edges would still touch and damage the drag strut retraction cylinders.

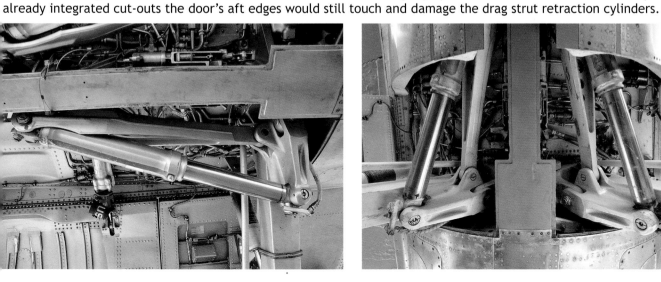

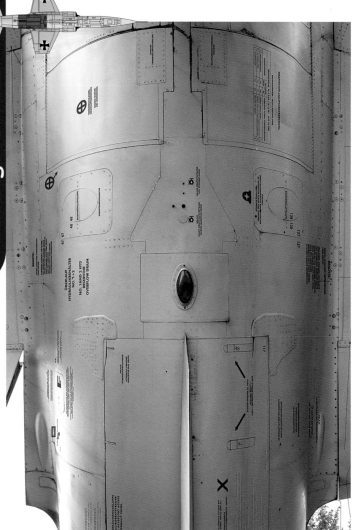

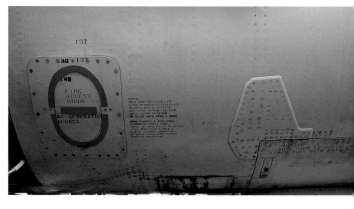

All German Starfighters are fitted with a second anti-collision beacon just in front of the ventral stabilization fin.

The lower fuselage is equipped with oval flapper doors similar to the doors on top of the fuselage to allow ground cooling and fire access to the engine bay.

The large hinged access door houses the aircraft hydraulic management center and is locked using four large latches. Note the reinforcement panels at the front door corners on the fuselage.

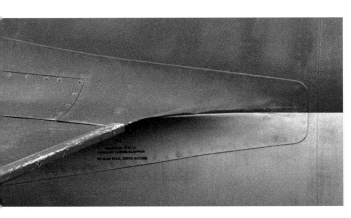

The external electrical power receptacle is located on the jet's right side, below the trailing edge of the wing.

The interphone jack connection is also located here, in the upper right corner.

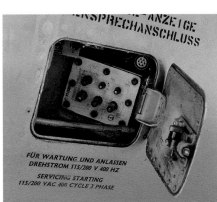

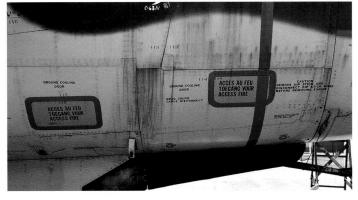

Three piano hinged flapper doors provide additional cooling air when the engine is running on the ground and give access to the engine bay for fire fighting. Note the stabilization fin with the lower TACAN / IFF (Identification of Friend or Foe) unpainted fiberglass antenna at its aft end.

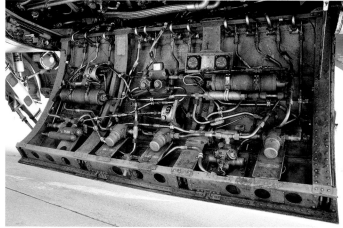

To make quick servicing on the F-104 an easy job, the hydraulic service panel allows access to the two separate systems, the No. 1 (left half) and No. 2 (right half). Note the dual sets of hydraulic pressure accumulators, oil filters, pressure regulators, pressure indicators, valves, tubing and external pressure rig connecting points. The red knobs in the centre are hydraulic fluid filler valves to which the hydraulic cart is connected.

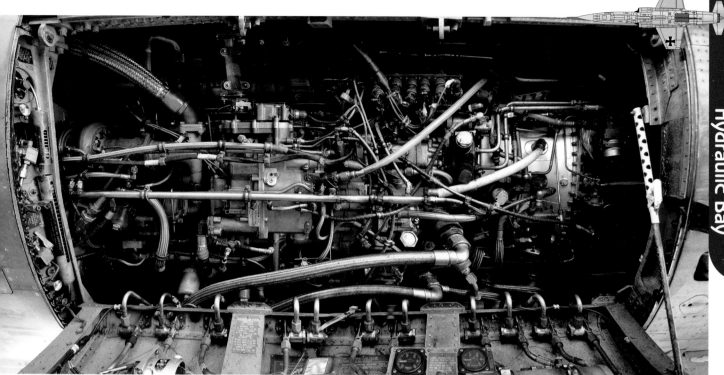

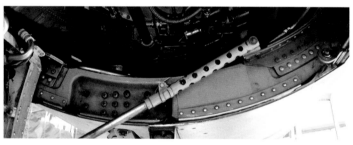

Looking upwards into the engine bay through the opened hydraulic service panel, one can see the engine's bottom with its various utilities, connecting tubing and wiring.

Two small horizontal tubes stand out when looking forward inside the fuselage rim: these are the No. 1 and No. 2 system hydraulic quantity indicators.

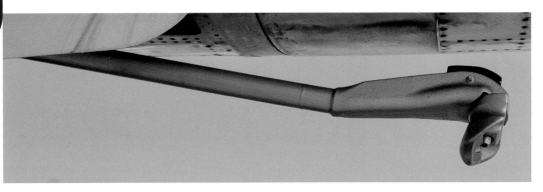

The F-104 is equipped with an arrestor hook to engage an airfield barrier during an emergency landing. The hook is released through pilot action. Its weight causes it to drop down and slide along on its bumper pad. Once released it is held down hydraulically and cannot be retracted without a technicians intervention.

The F-104 uses a drag chute during landing. When the pilot pulls the drag chute handle, the spring assisted bay opens and releases a small pilot chute followed by the main drag chute. The whole package is discarded at the end of the runway to be retrieved by the survival technicians.

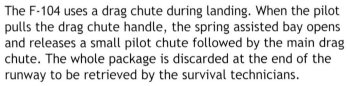

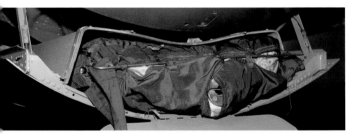

© Luc Van Grinderbeek

The arrester hook automatically lowers partially when the drag chute bay opens. The bay features a protection patch where it touches the hook. Note the drag chute door closing handle dangling from its groove in the lower fuselage, located just aft of the door.

ECM

As a countermeasure to the increasing threat of Soviet radar guided anti-aircraft SAM systems, the German Luftwaffe installed the EL-70 ECM system on their nuclear-role F-104Gs, consisting of an upper and lower cone shaped antenna. As with other ECM systems of those early days, this system got constantly adjustments resulting in updates like the EL-70B and EL-70C. But the EL-70 (even with its updates) quickly became obsolete and so some Luftwaffe Starfighters received the EL-73 ECM system, which consisted of a small antenna near the nose and a wig shaped housing with sensors aft of the parachute housing.

Manufactured by the Italian company Elettronica at Rome, 150 EL-70C and 112 EL-73 units have been installed on selected Fighter-Bomber Starfighters.

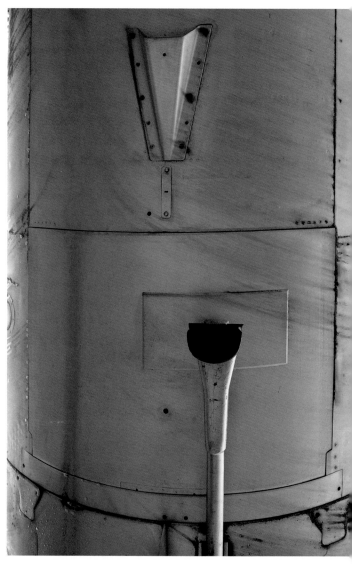

The Royal Dutch AF installed an US based ECM system on their Volkel stationed Recce and Fighter-Bomber (R)F-104Gs. This rounded-off wig housing is located at the same place as the German version and is installed together with the two sensors located near the radome.

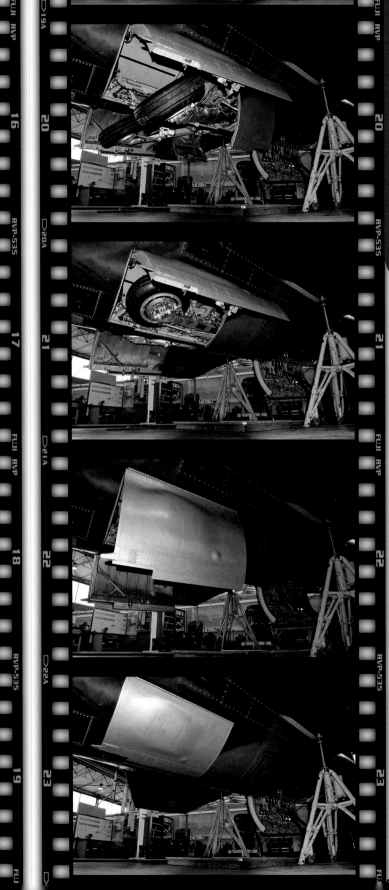

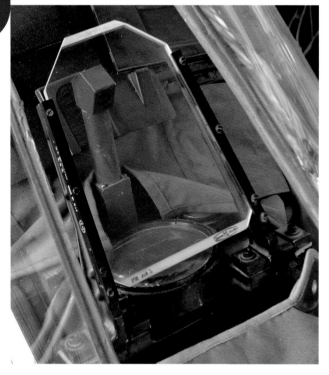

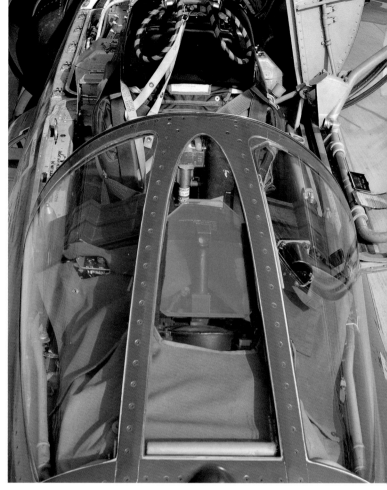

Front view of the optical sight combining glass to which all relevan flight data as well as the aiming reticle is projected through the round collimating lens underneath. The black device behind the glass is a periscope, which captures the projected information and the target viewed through the glass for recording by the gun camera

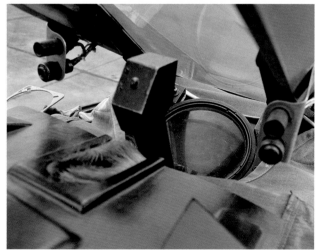

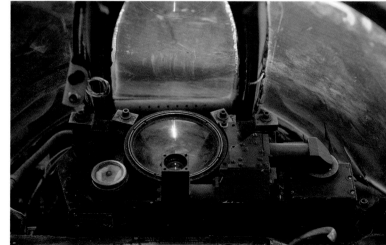

Two variations on the glare shield: pictures on the left depicting the Belgian/Dutch version, on the right the German version. Three top extensions can be pulled rearwards to provide the best shade conditions for reading the instruments. Below left are the standby compass and radar lock-on light behind it. Below right is the German combined EL-70/EL-73 ECM alert and failure lights. Inset is the original EL-70 version.

Above picture shows the general layout of the upper and lower instrument panel of a fighter-bomber F-104G. The upper panel protrudes slightly forward and groups all primary flight instruments, such as Mach/air speed, compass, AoA, attitude, turn & slip and rate of climb indicators, radio altimeter, accelerometer, altimeter, UHF selector and the German exclusive digital UHF channel display.

All essential engine parameter indicators are located on the right side.

The radarscope, which can be shielded with a visor as seen in the picture on the left, differs slightly between the interceptor and fighter-bomber versions.

The wheel-shaped landing gear selector is made of clear plastic and contains a red light that illuminates upon landing gear extension.

Above is the weapons selector panel, also showing the cannon rounds counter. Other indicators include landing gear safe 'green lights' and leading & trailing edge position markers. The above right picture shows the interceptor version of the fuel quantity panel with the radar mode lights below the radar antenna tilt indicator. The red emergency nozzle closure handle is used in case a loss of oil pressure, which causes the engine exhaust nozzle to fail in the open position, causing a loss of thrust.

Left is the special weapons selection panel and to the right of it the yellow canopy jettison handle.

71

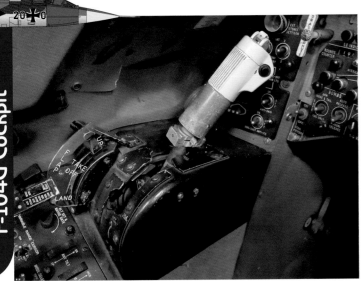

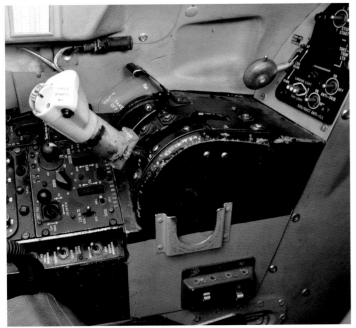

The throttle quadrant controls the engine RPM between idle and full military power, with detents for the fuel cut-off and the full afterburner positions. The handle also sports the speed brake and microphone switches. German F-104s also have a stow position for the MB ejection seat's safety harness central turnbuckle below the throttle.

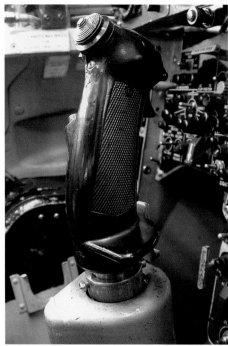

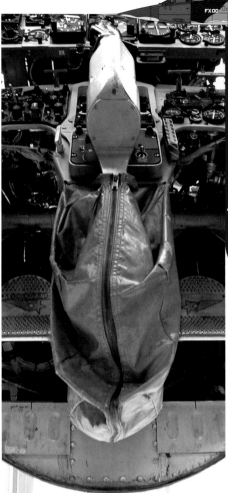

The stick is equipped with switches to control trim, the gun and communications. Below the stick is the shaker module that automatically vibrates fiercely when exceeding a certain AoA.

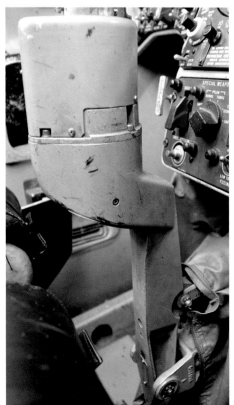

The adjustable foot pedals control the rudder and on the ground the wheel brakes. Note the Lockheed logo which has left and right versions.

The left cockpit console is equipped with various control panels, which differ between the German fighter-bomber version (top), the Dutch and Belgian FB versions (above — with a modification including a ground-speed selector, rearranging the autopilot control, the UHF radio control and the emergency UHF panels rearwards) and the interceptor version featuring the radar control panel with the radar positioning control 'joystick' (right).

A series of circuit breakers and switches is situated at the edge of this side panel.

Top left: The fighter-bomber version's left console, here with two range counters on the radar control panel. Top right: a similar view of the same console for the interceptor version.

Left picture shows the extra run-in timer installed in the Dutch recce RF-104G.

The black box on the right picture houses the emergency UHF comm battery pack. Also visible are the white cockpit floodlight and the detachable map reading light. Note the manufacturer's construction plate in the background.

The right console contains panels for the oxygen regulator, TACAN, IFF/SIF, dual run-in timers, the Position & Homing Indicator (PHI) navigation, C-2G compass and LN-3 inertial navigation alignment control.

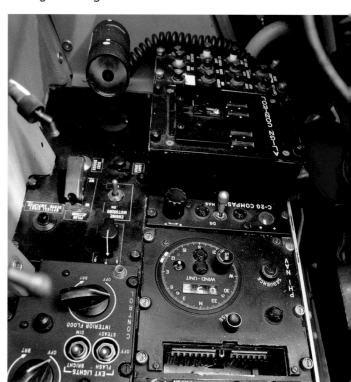

The pictures on this page depict four different right console variants of German Starfighters. As some panels are interchangeable, slight variations are possible. Especially the dual run-in timers and the PHI-NAV panel seem to have no standard location. German fighter-bombers have the ground-speed selector mounted on the right side wall.

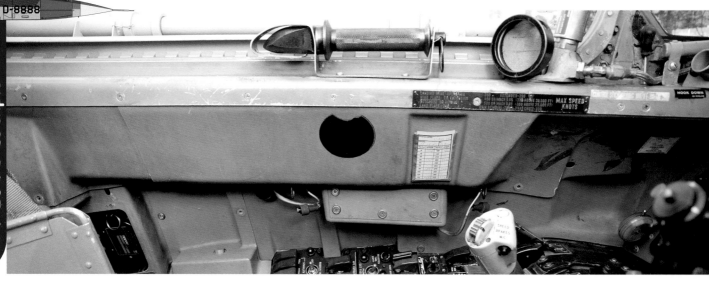

Top picture shows the canopy Plexiglas breaker knive and its holder sitting on top of the left cockpit wall. Just below it, next to the compass correction chart, is a black circular sticker, which the Dutch pilots use to blank off a defective flight instrument to avoid distraction. The aft side of the cockpit has two heating diffusers beside the ejection seat and on the left side the supply connection point for the defogging tubing.

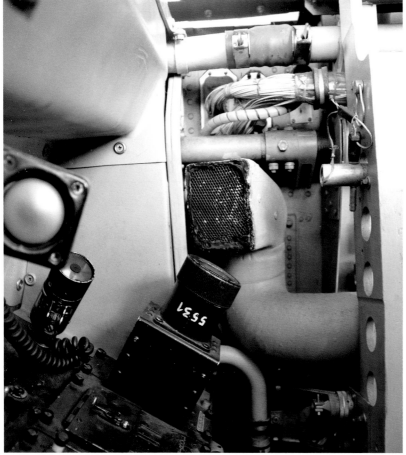

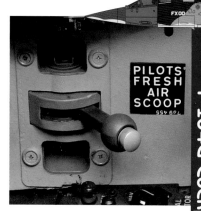

The pilot fresh air scoop located on the outside of the fuselage near the canopy unlock handle is opened from the inside by pushing the button and moving the handle forward. It allows fresh outside air to flow inside in case of smoke in the cockpit.

The yellow canopy internal locking lever, here on the left in unlocked position, is placed at the right forward side of the cockpit wall.

The pin on the locked position side activates the canopy unsafe warning light when it's not pushed in properly.

79

Two cartridge-actuated ejectors are located on the front left and right side of the canopy sills. These eject the canopy frame in case of an emergency. The knive-like canopy breaking tool can be used to cut the plexi-glass. Dutch F-104s have a stopwatch installed on the left canopy rim. The hook-down buttor (left German version) are also located on this side.

A canopy closing guide cam, two canopy lifter cams and three hidden locking hooks are integrated in the right cockpit rim.

© Luc Janssen

The canopy defogging pipes surround almost the entire canopy frame. The connection point is located in the aft lower left corner and makes contact upon canopy closure.

Left pictures show the connection in the Starfighter with C-2 ejection seat. Due to the different shaped Martin-Baker ejection seat in the German F-104s, this connection point has been relocated, as can be seen on the right pictures.

The defogging tubing also provides structural rigidity to the canopy, hence the U-shaped aft tube. During normal pressurized flight, small jets of warm air from the air-conditioning system are forced through perforated holes in the front and the two side tubes, to prevent fogging of the windshield and canopy interior surfaces.

Two mirrors are placed on the front defogging tube to 'check ones six'.

The right tube ends at a handle used by the pilot to open and close the canopy. A small lever is located just aft of this handle and with his thumb the pilot unlocks the canopy out of its full open position.

Front and aft view of the canopy's inner right side. Note the three locator pins, the canopy-opening handle and its unlocking lever.

A single cable runs from this lever alongside the aft tubing towards the locking hook, as shown below.

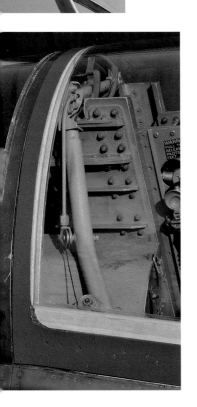

C-2 Ejection Seat

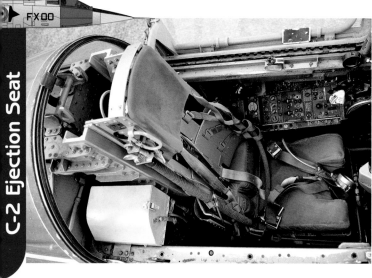
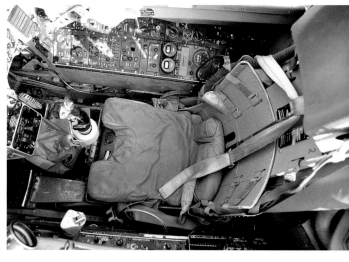

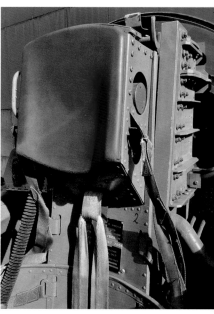

© Jan Govaerts

All F-104s were initially equipped with Lockheed-designed C-2 ejection seats. In case of ejection two side arms rotate forward, pulling out an arm-restraining harness. The grey letterbox-like device in the top left picture is a Dutch A.F. modification for stowing a gasmask.
For exercise debriefing purposes a camera in Belgian F-104s records images of the radarscope, by way of a mirror attached on the defogging tubes next to the pilot's head.

The survival kit doubles as a cushion. Cables connected to the typical F-104 'spurs' retract the pilot's feet to the seat in case of an ejection.

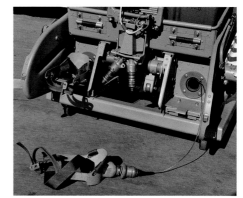

85

Between 1966 and 1968 German Air Force F-104s were re-equipped with British-build Martin-Baker Mk GQ7A zero-zero ejection seats. Among the other NATO's Starfighter operators only Denmark, Greece and Italy followed suit.

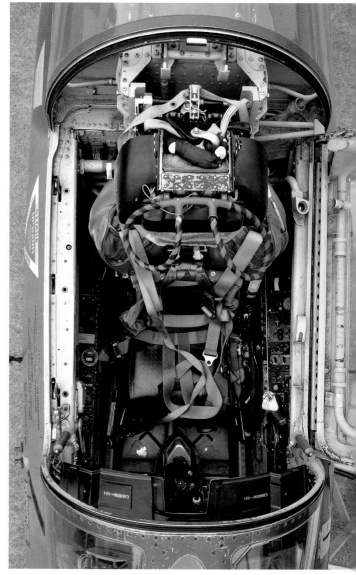

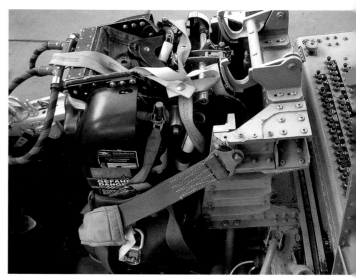

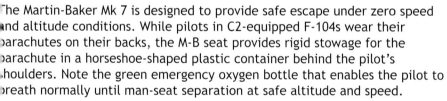

The Martin-Baker Mk 7 is designed to provide safe escape under zero speed and altitude conditions. While pilots in C2-equipped F-104s wear their parachutes on their backs, the M-B seat provides rigid stowage for the parachute in a horseshoe-shaped plastic container behind the pilot's shoulders. Note the green emergency oxygen bottle that enables the pilot to breath normally until man-seat separation at safe altitude and speed.

The canopy's rear glazing is incorporated in the electronic compartment hatch. Note the V-shaped reinforcement.

The black box on the left picture is the REU-10B technical malfunction registration box and is part of the LEADS 200 Flight Data recorder system found on some German F-104Gs.

An example of the F-104 easy-does-it design philosophy is all the electronics gear packaged in one conveniently arranged compartment, which can be reached simply by opening a hinged hatch.

The black box at left on the inside of the open hatch is part of the Position and Homing Indicator (PHI) that shows the pilot where he is by remembering where the flight started and keeping track of course changes, time and speed. The alert align unit, the smaller black box on the right, provides a QRA align capability for the LN-3 inertial platform in less than 2 1/2 minutes, provided the normal alignment of more than 10 minutes is performed beforehand.

Modular boxes containing all vita electronic equipme the so-called F-10 Jeep Cans, are quic replaced by a single technician thanks to their plug-in design. Just pullin on the T-handle disconnects the computer box.

The rim seal around the compartment inflates so this par of the fuselage ca be pressurized.

Note the hatch is always open during refueling to avoid build-up of kerosene fumes in this compartment.

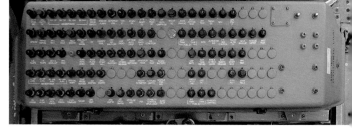

The typical circuit breaker box of the F-104 is situated in the front part of the electronics compartment, just behind the ejection seat. Different circuit breaker configurations can be found on this box.

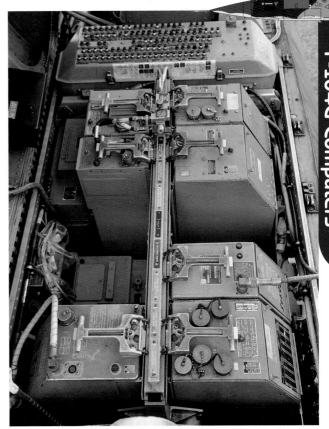

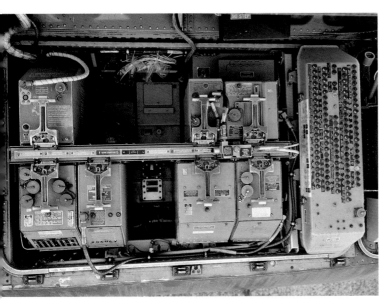

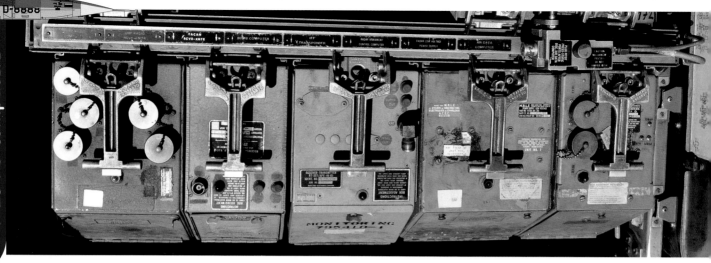

This page shows the nearest row of 'Jeep cans' in the electronics bay. Variations are possible dependent on fighter-bomber or interceptor versions.

From left to right: the autopilot computer, TACAN receiver-transmitter, IFF transponder, radar low voltage power supply and the electronic & calibration control amplifier.

All computers in this row have side covers that can be opened showing additional switches and testing connections inside.

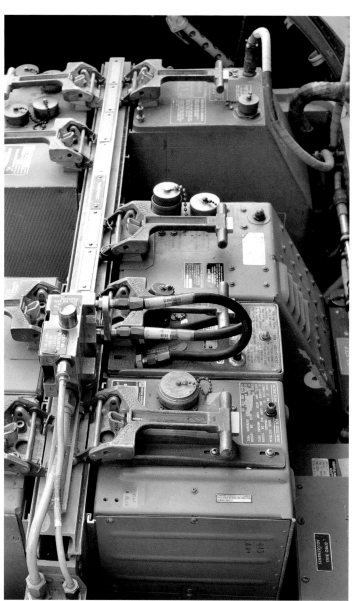

The furthermost row of electronics containers, from left to right: UHF receiver-transmitter, the much smaller bombing computer which is replaced by the Data link computer in the interceptor, the radar armament control computer, the air data computer and the inertial navigation computer.

Note the blue anodized connectors on the black hoses that link the air data computer to the Pitot tube.

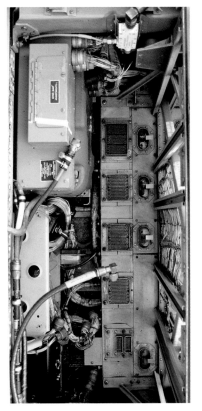

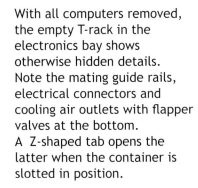

With all computers removed, the empty T-rack in the electronics bay shows otherwise hidden details. Note the mating guide rails, electrical connectors and cooling air outlets with flapper valves at the bottom.
A Z-shaped tab opens the latter when the container is slotted in position.

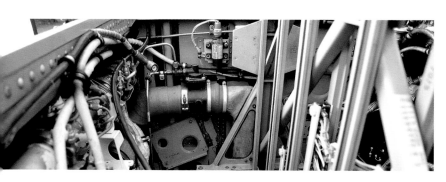

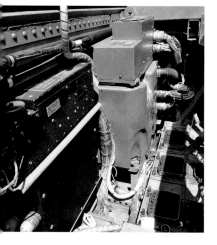

Situated in the left forward corner of the electronics bay is the Litton LN-3 inertial navigation platform, the grey boxes on the above left picture. A set of accelerometers and two gyros continuously determines the aircraft's position over any region of the earth's surface without emission or receipt of electromagnetic radiation. It senses the aircraft's attitude and provides this information to associated equipment, and determines ground track velocity for use by the ground speed error indicating system.

Picture below shows the containers without side covers; the smaller device in the foreground is the LN-3 inertial navigator platform without its blanket cover. Note the vacuum tube next to the radar low-voltage power supply computer, one of seven used within this container.

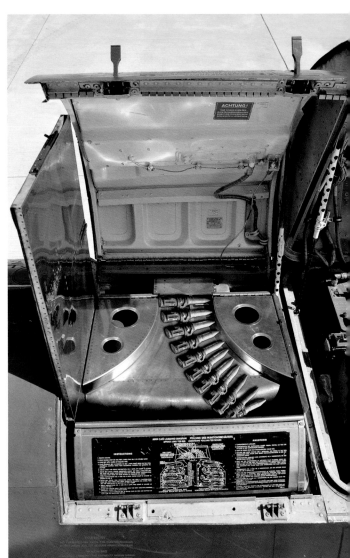

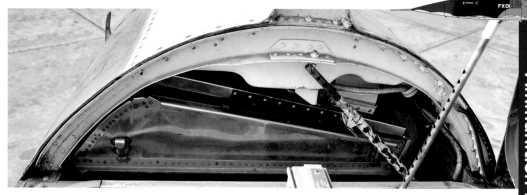

The ammunition box just behind the electronic compartment holds up to 750 rounds of 20 mm electrically primed shells for the M61A1 Vulcan Gatling cannon.
Spent cartridges are collected in the cartridge bay, a compartment located below the ammo box bay (see p.46), while the links are ejected overboard or retained together with the empty shells in the cartridge bay. In the latter case the limited capacity of the cartridge bay reduces the maximum ammunition load to 420 rounds.

© Robert Roggeman

Vertical shelves divide the box into three compartments and horizontal shelves keep the linked bullet layers separated during aircraft maneuvering as well as firing.

An ammo loader can be hung on the fuselage to make loading easier.

The TF-104 is a fighter serving double duty as a trainer. The two-seat Starfighter has the same flight characteristics as the single-seater. It flies as fast and as high and it climbs as quickly. The TF carries the same fire control, communication and navigation systems as the F-104G and can fly missions with Sidewinders, unguided rockets and bombs under its wings. Both cockpits of the TF-104G are fitted with exactly the same controls and instrument displays as the F-104G and can be flown from either cockpit.

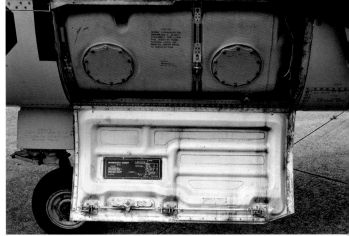

The TF-104 has no provision for the Vulcan cannon.
The gun compartment of the single-seater is used for an
internal auxiliary fuel tank containing an extra 150 liters.
The standard gun access panel opens up to the aft part of
the auxiliary fuel tank.
Picture above of the German F-104F gun muzzle cover
shows its similarity to the earlier F-104D version.

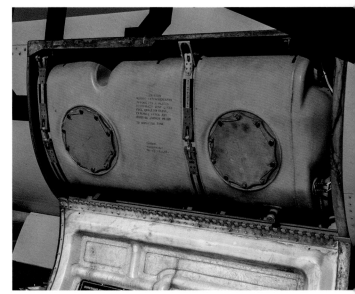

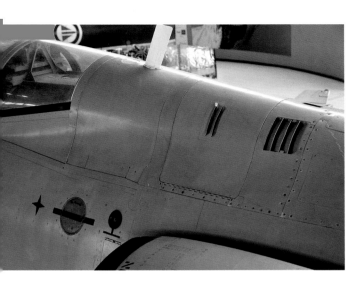

The TF-104G's single pressure refueling point is situated at approximately the same position as on the F-104G. As with the single-seater, the electronics bay cover must be opened before single-point refueling starts to prevent buildup of fumes in this compartment.

The single-seater's front gravity refueling point is absent in this area while the aft point remains in the same position in the back near the wing root.

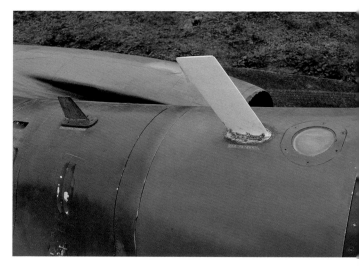

The two antennas on top of the TF-104's electronics bay hatch are the UHF antenna (big white) and the smaller IFF antenna. On the F-104G these antennas are integrated into and flush with the spine.

Note the cooling air scoop for the TF electronics compartment, located more to the aft compared to the F-104G. The single external locking handle unlocks and locks both canopies at the same time.

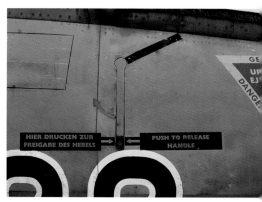

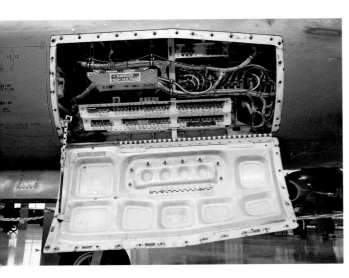

The two-seater's circuit breaker bay is located below the cockpit. The green Liquid Oxygen converter bottle contains ten liters, double the amount of the single-seater for obvious reasons. The Ram Air Turbine is extended in case of emergency to provide hydraulic pressure and electric power. The pump and its connections are visible behind the extended RAT.

Two individual cockpit lower access hatches are situated below the ejection seats. These hatches have no function in the ejection system but serve as the primary means of removing and installing the seats during maintenance.

The front cockpit access hatch can be removed completely from the fuselage in the same manner as on the single-seater. The aft hatch hinges at the aft end and gives access to two horizontally mounted Jeep cans. Due to the lack of space in the main electronics bay the Armament Control computer and the Radar low voltage power supply units have been relocated to this place under the aft seat.

The TF's nose landing gear is relocated to the front of the NLG well and retracts aft. Its torque scissors now point forward. The gear doors are rectangular, missing the triangular cable deflectors.

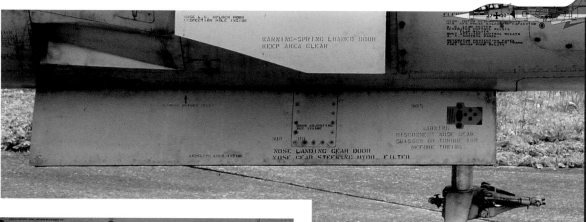

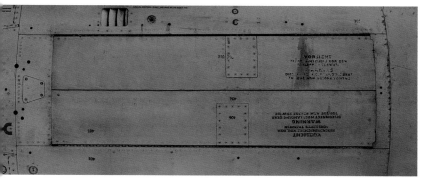

The inside of the TF-104 nose gear bay; prominent in these pictures is the lower drag link connected to its double upper part, which by means of the actuating cylinder retracts the whole NLG, and the locking cam.

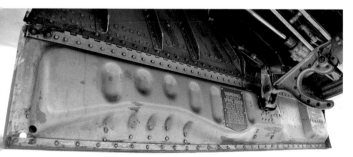

The inside of the TF-104 nose gear well doors, showing how their internal shape differs from the single-seaters. The left and right doors also differ from one other. The area behind the intakes is almost the same for both versions, the TF having no internal well for the centerline pylon and as such is not capable of carrying this pylon.

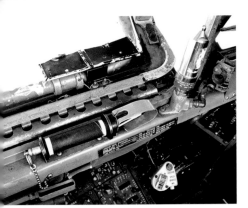

The front cockpit in the TF-104 is primarily for the student pilot flying in VFR conditions with the instructor occupying the aft cockpit.

This cockpit is equipped with an optical sight and has all the standard controls required for weapon delivery. The lower part of the control stick column is typical for the TF's front cockpit and quite different from the single-seat version resembling the original F-104A/B/C/D assembly.

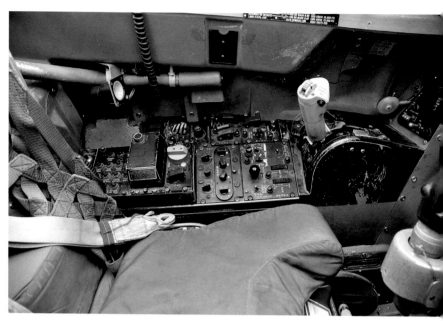

The left side panels in the TF-104 front cockpit can differ in the same way as the single-seaters with systems installed according to the needs of the various users. Note the emergency UHF radio with its black battery pack.

The right side panels of the TF's front office. Note the dual timer in the photo above used for delivery of a nuclear store. This Lear manufactured timing device replaces the original Mergenthaler Linotype M-2 bombing computer.

The front C-2 seat is equipped with two spikes on top to break the canopy glass in case the hood is not blown off moments before ejection. Norwegian TFs have different shaped canopy breakers on their front seats

Front and rear cockpits in the TF-104G are separated by a Plexiglas plate, preventing air streaming in the aft cockpit after the front canopy is blown off and flames entering when the front ejection seat is activated.

Top picture shows the sizes of the internal mirrors to good advantage. In the front canopy they are noticeably smaller than in the rear. Note also the rather tight fit of the defogging tube in the front hood, coinciding closely with the curvatures of the glass.

113

The main instrument panel in the TF-104 aft cockpit is quite similar to the one in the front except that the armament panel (left of the radarscope) lacks all selection switches.

A khaki coloured canvas covering the area between the cockpits protects the back of the aft cockpit instruments

Typical in Dutch TF-104s is the stopwatch case next to the left side canopy jettison explosive charge, empty in the left picture. The forked canopy guide in the aft cockpit is noticeably different from that in the front: higher and slightly less curved. On the other hand, the aft control stick is identical, typical of all US-built Starfighters.

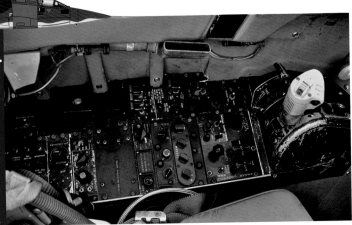

Photos of the aft cockpit left and right consoles of the Dutch (top) and Norwegian (above) showing their minor differences. Note the closed top of Norwegian aft C-2, along with the canopy lifters and locking points on the right rim.

The aft canopy is equipped with a stowage box containing the black curtain for covering-off the pilot's view while practicing Instrument Flight Rules (IFR) flying. Two guiding rails support the deployed curtain.

The air conditioning bay and the aft electronics compartment on the TF-104, together in the picture below. Note the typical Jeep cans, similar to the ones in the single-seater. From top to bottom: inertial navigation computer, TACAN radar receiver/transmitter and the electronic & calibration control amplifier computer. The black box on the inside of the cover is the missile in-range computer.

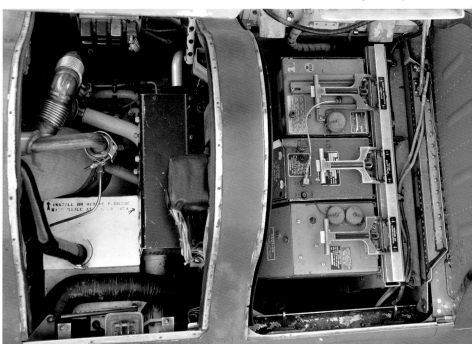

The forward electronics compartment contains three Jeep cans, from left to right the air data computer, IFF radio (not installed) and UHF radio. Note the circuit breaker & junction box in front of them and the PHI navigation computer on the inside of this compartment's cover. The Litton LN-3 inertial navigator platform is located just beside the air data computer.

The last part of the two-seater canopies is integrated with the fwd electronics bay hatch, as can be seen from the picture above.

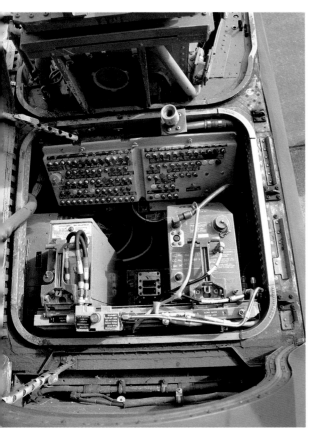

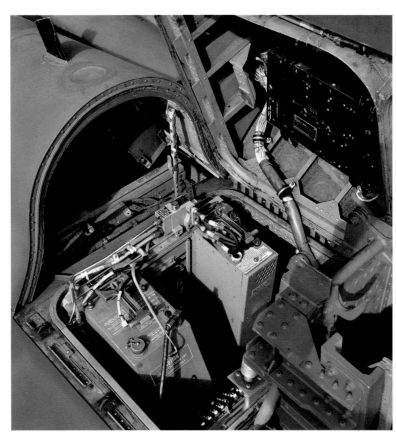

Front cockpit of the F-104F. Thirty examples of this variant were hastily produced by Lockheed for the Bundesluftwaffe to allow pilot training to begin, awaiting the introduction of the TF-104G. Based on the F-104D, the F-model lacks fire control system and radar, hence the absence of radar screens in both cockpits.

The aft cockpit of the
F-104F looks as bare as
the front, being restricted
to flight instruments only
and devoid of armament
control systems. Note the
clipboard instead of the
usual radarscope. The
instruments are basically
the same as on the F-104D.
A noticeable difference with
the TF-104G is the curved
one-piece glare shield.

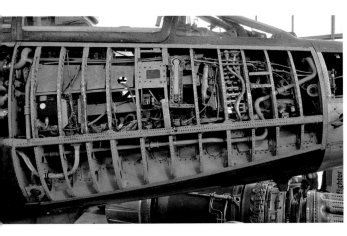

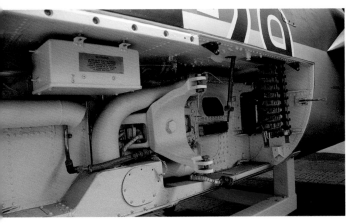

The skinned Starfighter reveals its bones. Of interest is the empty Vulcan gun compartment showing the otherwise hidden used cartridge and link ejection chutes, discharging in the shell case stowage compartment. The picture below shows the forward boresight target-aligning fixture deployed. The aft can be seen in picture above.

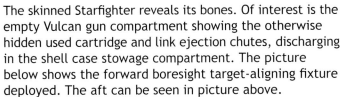

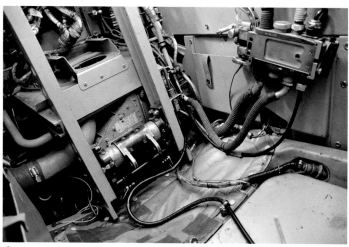

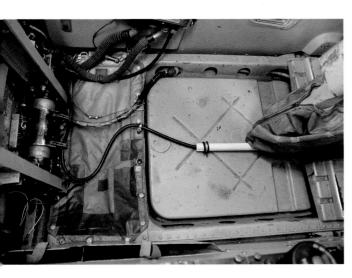

Most pictures on the previous page show all sides of the cockpit with the ejection seat removed.

The picture below shows ground crew removing the lower cockpit access hatch, alowing the unusual pictures on the right, revealing the bottom of the Martin-Baker seat (top) and the canvas covered stick shaker assembly.

Note the white protection tube around the wire leading to the lower UHF antenna integrated in this hatch.

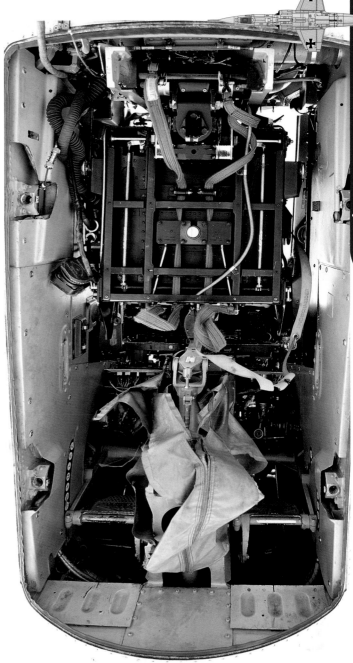

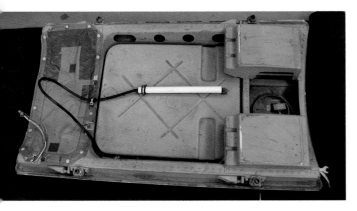

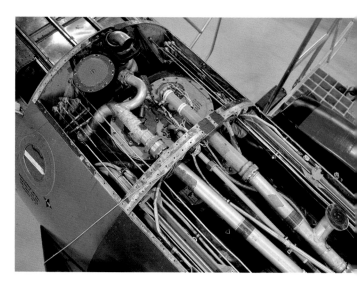

With the dorsal access panels removed, ten control cable and the fuel transfer piping running through the spine of this German Starfighter come to light.

Beneath these pipes are the auxiliary (front) and the forward main fuselage bladder fuel tanks, of which the yellow zinc chromate 'manhole covers' stand out.

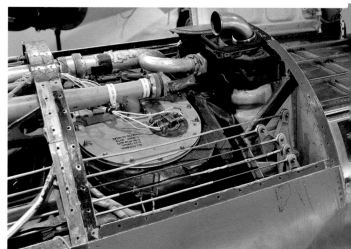

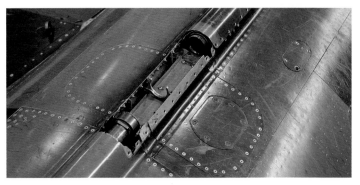

A F-104 cut in half shows the inside of the main bladder tank with its two fuel pumps and piping on the bottom. These pumps are accessible from the belly of the aircraft, as can be seen in the pics below. The rubber bladder is attached to the inside skin of the Starfighter's fuselage. Piping from the heat exchanger runs through the spine.

The transitional space between the fuselage and wing houses the five wing-root forgings along with the leading and the trailing edge flap actuators. Both actuators are electrically operated in contrast with the hydraulic powered aileron servos fitted near the center of the wing.

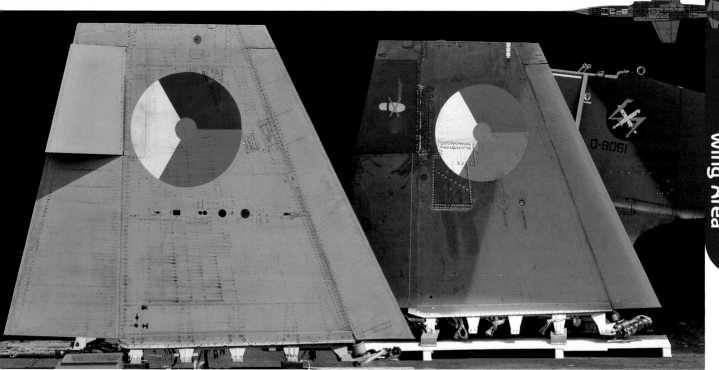

The thin F-104 wing is not designed to carry internal fuel. Root and tip forgings in combination with 12 channel-section stiffeners form a strong torsion box to which lower and upper skins are riveted. These rivet dents are then puttied over before painting to obtain a smooth wing surface.

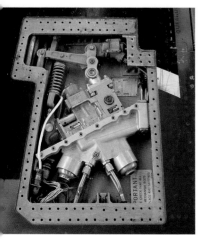

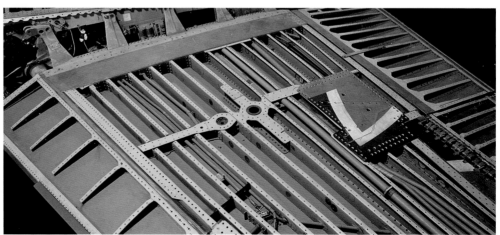

Close-ups of the nose (left) and wing jacks (above).

Access to the engine is greatly simplified by removal of the entire tail unit, weighing 600 kilos, which is positioned on a transportation dolly and held in position with four retaining cables.

Removing panels 79 and 102 reveals the stabilizer servo assembly squeezed in the front part of the vertical tail. Movements of the stick are transferred via cables along the fuselage to this unit where they are boosted by hydraulics. Right picture shows the disconnection point for the four hydraulic lines. And below is the rudder actuator assembly stored behind panel 86.

With the J-79 removed internal details of the engine bay emerge such as the secondary intake air bypass assembly bolted to the intake ducts. It consists of ten individual flaps, eight fixed and two operable, which control the flow of intake-duct air around the engine. The empty shroud houses the starter motor of the J-79, driven by compressed air from a GSE unit connected to its receptacle in the right main wheel bay.

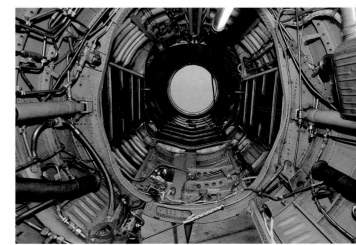

The J-79 engine is hung by two mounts on a simple rail. The forward mount consists of a dual roller by which the engine can be easily slide in and out. Additionally these rollers allow expansion of the engine due to rising temperatures. The aft mounting consists of a wedge assembly that is hooked into a fuselage catch and bolted tight. The J-79 is also bolted to two side mounts (middle picture below).

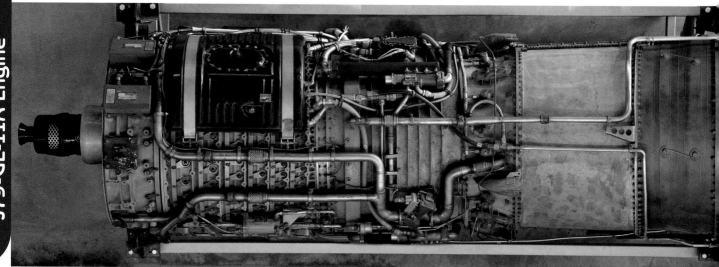

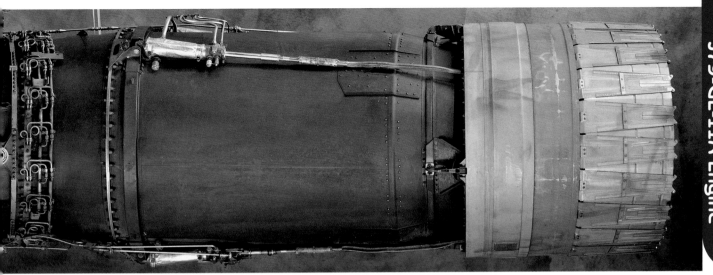

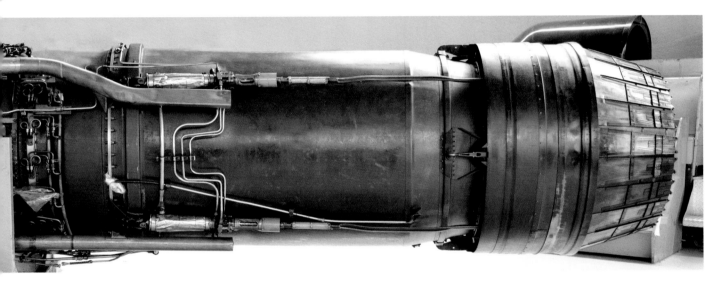

These spreads show the standard J-79-GE-11A's top, left and right sides.
The 1960 unit price of US$ 170,000 would amount to US$ 1,300,000 or around 1,000,000 euros in today's currency.

These pages reveal the details of the upgraded German built J-79-MTU-J1K engine. Besides the different exhaust nozzles note the subtle differences in the oil tank.

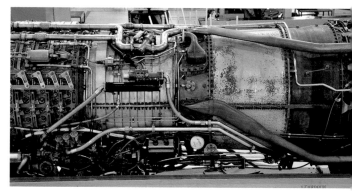

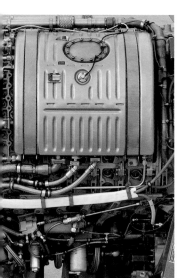

A collection of Ground Support Equipment (GSE), known as 'the train', is associated with starting up the Starfighter. Amongst them is a generator unit to supply electrical power and a massive air compressor to wind the engine turbine to 3,500 rounds per minute through the starter air connection located in the main wheel bay.

The F-104 with all its usual protective covers and Remove Before Flight tags. A fully dressed Starfighter carries 36 RBF flags in different sizes and colours.

© Daniel Brackx collection

© Eric Tammer

© Johan Bringmans

Four versions of the air intake covers are available: the left cover has an extendable cotton sleeve for connecting a ground heating unit to preheat the engine and oil systems in freezing winter conditions. The meshed air scoop screen (below left) is fitted while running up the engine for maintenance.

The typical Starfighter access ladder is used by all F-104 operating NATO allies and has afterwards often been reduced by one step for use with the F-16A/B, the F-104G's successor.

© Jan Govaerts

139

The fighter QRA at Beauvechain AB in Belgium at night: two pairs of Zippers ready to take off at the sound of the bell.

The next pages deal with the wide variety of armament the Starfighter is capable of delivering, including the three different versions of 'special' (nuclear) weapons that the F-104G has carried, the main reason the German government pushed Lockheed for the development of its beefier F-104 version.

© Flor De Neve collection

Armament

141

© Jan Govaerts

The standard interceptor armament on European Starfighters consists of two Sidewinders on wingtip-mounted Red Dog launchers, on this page the AIM-9B model. The green body of the Bravo above is an attempt to blend the missile in with the Belgian camouflage. The cut-open Bravo below shows the guidance and control section in the nose section, the guidance fins and the (yellow painted) warhead. The fins at the rear provide aerodynamic stability, but it is the 'rollerons' at their ends providing gyroscopic precession that prevents the serpentine motion that gave the Sidewinder its name.

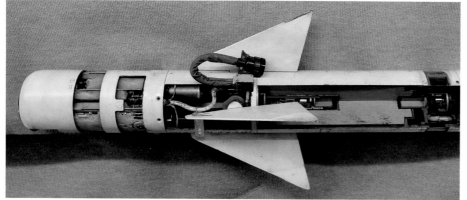

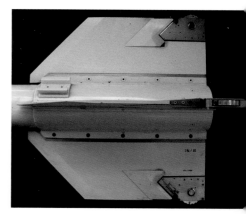

The first true dogfight Sidewinder, the AIM-9J/N, superseded the early Bravos in most of the F-104 fleets. This version can quickly be distinguished from the AIM-9B by its forward fins as seen on this page. Aircraft built for the Military Assistance Program (MAP), including all Lockheed-built TF-104s, can launch Sidewinders from AERO 3B launchers mounted to under wing pylons, as shown by the Norwegian dual seater below.

© Joop Dionet

All F-104s are wired to fire AIM-9s from the 'catamaran' installation consisting of two AERO 3B launchers attached to the belly pylon and most Starfighter operators made use of this provision.

One notable exception was the Belgian Air Force, which only briefly experimented with these belly launchers. Pictures of BAF F-104s in this configuration such as FX45 on the next page are therefore rather rare.

© Jin-De Shin

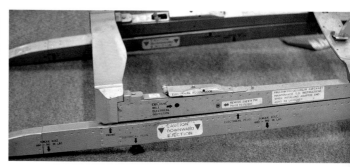

© Arie Kraak - NIMH

The German Navy chose the French Nord-Aviation AS.20 (above) and improved AS.30 (below) as air-to-ship/air-to-ground missiles for the F-104G, awaiting the more capab home-bred Kormoran, similar to the famous Exocet.

With the range of 13 km, the AS guided rockets are capable of taking out small to medium-sized warships. However, to successfully engage the target the F-104 has to follow the missile to within 3 km of the target, which is rather a drawback, while the pilot visually steers the missile by remote radio control, assisted by one or more tail-mounted flares.

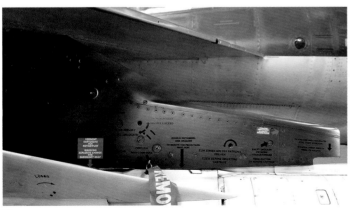

Two starting rockets plus one propulsive rocket engine accelerate the AS.30 to supersonic speed, after which th 230 kg warhead impacts at about 500 m/sec - 1800 km/h

Note the adapted wing pylon, redesigned to carry the AS. and AS.30, as well as their successor the AS-34 Kormoran-

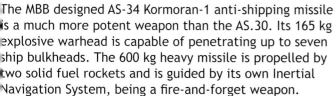

The MBB designed AS-34 Kormoran-1 anti-shipping missile is a much more potent weapon than the AS.30. Its 165 kg explosive warhead is capable of penetrating up to seven ship bulkheads. The 600 kg heavy missile is propelled by two solid fuel rockets and is guided by its own Inertial Navigation System, being a fire-and-forget weapon.

The Twin Store Carrier (TSC), is only mounted under the wings and allows carrying a doub[?] load of bombs o[?] rocket pods.

Also part of the Starfighter's regular weapon[?] are the Mk 82 Snakeye and BL755 cluster bomb, which seven bays contain 147 anti-personnel submunitions wit[?] or without chut[?]

© Wilfried Zetsche

© Daniel Brackx collection

© Jos Schoofs

The cluster bomb submunition with 'star' tail section.

© Jos Van Nes collection

© KB Air Museum

© Daniel Brackx collection

LAU-32 and LAU-3A rocket pods contain respectively 7 and 19 2.75 inch Mk 4 Folding Fin Aerial Rockets (FFAR). Originally intended as an air-to-air weapon, these unguided rockets were later developed into a modular rocket for air-to-ground use.

NUR FÜR-BDU-33B/B ODER-DM18
2 JABO G 34 ELOWA STAFFEL
4

NUR FÜR-BDU-33B/B ODER-DM18
JABO G 34 ELOWA STAFFEL
3

The German Mk 25 Ubungsbombenträger (Practise bomb dispenser) carrying two BDU-33 25-lb practise bombs on the front store and two BDU-48 10-lb on the aft. Both Bomb Dummy Units (BDU) simulate free fall aerial bomb deliveries. The BDU-33 simulates the toss/loft and dive deliveries of a nuclear store or a low drag Mk 82 GP bomb. The BDU-48 simulates the trajectory of a retarded nuclear bomb during a lay-down (level) delivery thanks to its blunt front end, low weight and box-type fin.

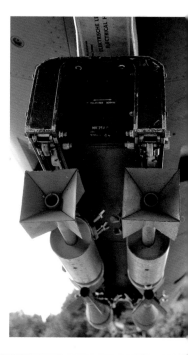

20✠57

The Rocket-Bomb-Dispenser is a unique Dutch designed carrier for four 2.75 inch FFAR training rockets in combination with four BDU-33/Mk 76 or BDU-48/Mk 106 practise bombs.

The rockets can be fired in ripple or individually.

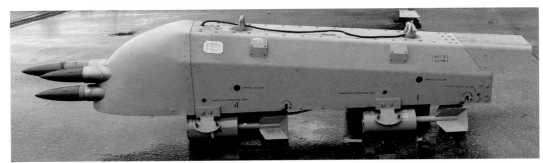

The Belgian Air Force uses the Mk 25 Bomb Rack adapter, a simple U-shaped bomb dispenser for its practise bombs until the arrival of the SUU-21/A container. Note the small fairing on the front face of the centre pylon. Both types of BDU are fitted with a type Mk4 Mod 3 smoke cartridge in the nose. Upon impact, the firing pin impacts the signal cartridge cap, which ignites a red phosphorous charge creating a yellow flash. White smoke is then expelled through the rear part of the tail tube, thus allowing observation of the impact point.

© Didier Waelkens

The SUU-21/A practise bomb dispenser is regularly mounted on Belgian and German F-104s to train the delivery of 'special weapons', aka nuclear bombs. The dispenser can carry up to six 25-lb practise bombs in a forward and an aft bomb bay, complete with their associated doors. These doors were added on the SUU-21/A to prevent inadvertent bomb release over the populated areas of Europe.

© Robert Roggeman

© Willy Peeters

After the UN convention of 1980 banned the use of napalm bombs, most of the disused BLU-1 and -27 canisters are converted into travel pods. The BLU-1 nose and tail are a smooth ogive shape, while the BLU-27s are much more angular in appearance.

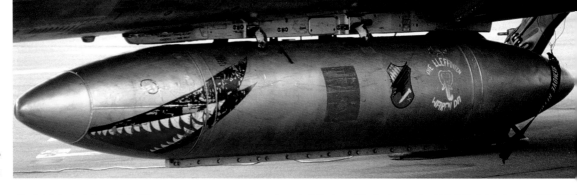

The German Marine used a converted F-84 fuel tank to transport mail to the 'shooting camps' on Deci air base in Sardinia, appropriately painted in the colours of Deutsche Post.

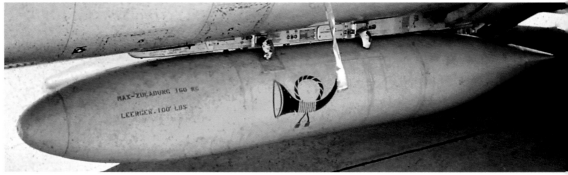

154

The Dutch developed Orpheus reconnaissance pod housing five daylight Oldelft cameras is used for high-speed low-altitude recce work. Using film speeds matching perfectly the aircraft speed, which results in very sharp pictures, it also features an Infra Red Line Scanner and a Coupler Control Unit. The pod is also used under their F-16s.

© Joop Dionet

Widely used with the F-104 is the A/A37U-15 Dart Gunnery Aerial Target, manufactured by Del Mar Engineering Company, and consisting of a RMU-10/A reeling unit and a TDU-10/B target. The wooden target, covered by an aluminium alloy skin, is mounted with its reeling pod under the F-104's left wing pylon. This installation has to be counterbalanced with a full fuel tank under the right wing pylon.

© Joop Dionet

The Dart is towed approximately 700 m behind and 150 m below the Starfighter and is released at the end of the mission and recovered by a parachute. Because the target often behaves erratically while in the air, the Belgian Air Force gave up this particular system after just a few tests and went looking for another system...

Because of its more docile behavior the Belgian Air Force preferred the French designed Secapem aerial target for air-to-air gunnery training. Two Secapem type 520 containers are carried, one under each wing.

© Jan Govaerts

The left container remains empty, while the right contains the dart shaped, visual augmenter and radar reflector Tetraplan, constructed from ladder-proof nylon mesh panels, with its towing cable. Target and cable are released at the end of the mission. Note the bright orange painted half of the tip tanks associated with BAF target towing F-104s.

© Willy Peeters

157

The Royal Dutch Air Force used a modified Secapem system, which combined a CTB-25 reeling unit under the right wing pylon with a thinner CTB-30 launching tube under the left wing. When not deployed, the cable between the reeling unit and the target dart is passing through a clip mounted just below the engine exhaust.

© Arie Kraak

© Joop Dionet

© Joop Dionet